LET THEM TEACH!

LET THEM TEACH!

The Laymen's Guide to Return Dignity to the Public Schools

by

Donald P. Schneider

Philosophical Library
New York

Library of Congress Cataloging in Publication Data

Schneider, Donald P. (Donald Paul), 1923-
    Let them teach!

    1. Public schools--United States. I. Title.
LA217.S29   371'.01'0973   80-84376
ISBN 0-8022-2382-6   AACR2

Manufactured in the United States of America

Overseas distributor: George Prior Ltd.
52-54 High Holborn, London WC1V 6RL

CONTENTS

PREFACE

There is a concern among all citizens that the public school systems are going downhill rapidly. The gradual lowering of standards began in the mid-1960s and there is no end in sight. Someone must put an end to this travesty of education.

Many students are pleased with this new permissiveness and at times they enjoy being able to be disruptive; however, most teachers in the schools today realize that education should not be this way.

The disruptive students are putting teachers' backs to the walls. Laymen must pressure boards of education to adopt the policies that will return stability to the public school classroom environment.

Public school education will continue along its downward course until laymen demand changes. Frankly, I wonder how most board of education members can sleep. If they really do not understand that most students are not in classes conducive to learning, then reading this manuscript will alert them.

Many poor decisions have been made in education. Board of education members must establish new policies and insist that all members of the management team and teaching staffs abide by policy.

The public school system should be respected, but the people who have attended good schools realize that something is missing in schools today. Pessimists contend that nothing can be done. Optimists hope that someone will do something. Realists understand that there are solutions, but someone must lead. Administrators, college professors, and school board members have usually failed. The laymen who have courage and common sense will not fail.

We will go on a quick tour in a time machine!

1932, 1942, 1952

The bell rang! Today we will develop sentences for the five vocabulary words that you are placing in your notebooks; we will review verb tenses; and then we will discuss the writing styles of two great writers of mystery, namely, your favorites and mine, Dashiell Hammett and Agatha Christie.

Please pass your homework papers to the front of the room.

John, use the first vocabulary word in a sentence.

1968, 1978, 1980

Come on, class. You heard the bell. Will you guys stop talking and get in your seats? Mary, turn off that radio. I told you guys to stay away from those windows. We're not going to start class until everyone is quiet.

Will you boys in the front get the books from the closet?

Bill, keep your hands to yourself. If you don't settle down soon, we'll return the books and you'll write all period.

The illustrations are not exceptions; rather, they are typical of the classroom behavior then and now. This is not to say that all teachers will experience this behavior each day. Some students will disrupt any classroom, and we are fortunate that these students are not in every classroom.

Some teachers instruct in the elective areas where the content is usually too difficult for disruptive students; other teachers are not as lucky.

In the mid-1960s the hippie movement greatly impeded education. The hippies decided that they were bored. They were bored because they were "too stoned" to study. The "do gooders" blamed the teaching techniques, and the search was on for entertainers, not teachers! Many students are looking to be entertained, not taught.

We must implement sound policies. We must also separate disruptive students from students who are in school to learn. Those who will not cooperate in alternative classes must be removed from public schools.

INTRODUCTION

On Thursday, July 5, 1979, Willard McGuire, president of the National Education Association, deplored the fact that thousands of teachers were leaving the teaching profession because of the stress associated with the many problems that confront teachers daily in their teaching and related assignments.

Some of the more prevalent stresses are related to violence, vandalism, disruptive students, inadequate salaries, demanding parents, fear, insecurity, and other high pressure situations. Teachers need help now.

For the millions of people who read those comments there are understandably varied reactions. As usual some readers will assume this to be a normal outcome because they experience the same stresses in their work; they hope that the teachers' association or union will be able to alleviate many of the problems. Other readers will believe that the problems are insurmountable, that life will continue to get worse, not better. Others who are concerned might talk to some friends in education, and others who are less concerned will return to other priorities.

As an educator who has taught English, health, physical education, reading, world history, American history, and math, coached five varsity athletic teams, and served as an administrator during the last thirty-two years, it is most urgent that I relate and recommend to you, the responsible citizen, that you can effect the vital changes that must begin immediately.

As you continue to read you will discover that you have the answers to correct our educational dilemma and that you need not fear the stock reply that quickly informs you that the important matter of education must be left to the professional.

The various problems involved will be analyzed in the chapters that follow. Sufficient depth will be provided for you to obtain a reasonable knowledge of the stress that a teacher experiences daily.

There will be no attempt to whitewash the fact that some teachers in the public schools have made no concerted effort to improve their teaching performances. These teachers, however, have been hired by administrators and supervisors and have been allowed to remain stationary or to slip backward in the profession because the management team has determined other duties to be more important.

Inflation and energy shortages are important concerns for all citizens. Citizens are pawns of the government in these areas, but public school education can be changed by a person who has enough interest to call a board of education member with a legitimate concern.

Almost daily you can read in newspapers and magazines about education programs being used. What the press publishes as news numerous other school districts were using twenty or thirty years ago. The public has no conception of what is actually taking place in public school education today. Publishers have printed educational material in expensive textbooks primarily for the teachers, supervisors, administrators, and librarians who might wish to use them professionally. Occasionally a book is published that will attempt to explain why students can't read, how to get your abdominal muscles in shape, or why jogging might be hard on females, but publishers have not taken a positive step in making it known to all citizens of the United States that laymen can exert pressure on their local board of education to adopt educational policies that will require all administrators and supervisors to improve the teaching performances of all personnel, to provide methods for removing disruptive students from the classrooms, and to consider other policies to protect the health and safety of the students.

The reader who is familiar with the major faults of education and the solution to the problems is better informed than the millions of people presently involved in education who are permitting conditions to deteriorate daily.

The community will suffer when it permits narrow-minded school board members to *rubber stamp*. Members, instead, should make decisions concerning policies, personnel, budget, pupil services, curricula, and transportation. Until board members are persuaded to obtain the facts and to vote independently, the administration and central office will be so busy trying to gather information impressive enough to snow-job the board that school personnel will not have sufficient time, direction, or support to run the schools properly.

Citizens believe that they understand what the problems are, but when they become school board members they suddenly become puppets! Day-to-day problems are to be decided by school personnel, but it is essential that the laymen set policies to provide the most conducive teaching/learning environment, one free from disturban-ces.

The solutions offered in this volume must be im-plemented immediately. They will give needed support to those people who realize that changes must be made and that the problems are far from insurmountable.

LET THEM TEACH!

VIOLENCE

Many studies, surveys, and personal observations show that violence has been increasing in the schools, elementary and intermediate as well as secondary.

Violence is present in various degrees of severity. Students have used desks, chairs, knives, razors, guns, combs, brushes, chains, boards, rocks, etc. in efforts to hurt persons in authority. Secretaries and other students have also been victims of similar violent attacks. These attacks do not always occur in isolated areas. Many occur in the office or just outside the door.

Other forms of violence that are not as physical but could easily become physical are those forms which students use as scare tactics. Verbal abuse in legal terms implies that a student intends to inflict immediate physical harm on another person, and, even though a teacher is not physically abused, there is the ever present threat that some students will react physically if their idea of freedom or manhood is in any manner denied them. Some students are very effective in using a stare, a sneer, or other

1

facial expressions which indicate to the teacher that the students can become violent whenever provoked even inadvertently.

Can you imagine going into a classroom five or six periods a day and having students prone to violence in two or more of those classes? As a teacher you are required to go into those classrooms five days a week.

It is true that many teachers are physically capable of handling themselves in most situations, but you must also remember that a student is not going to be realistic when he turns violent; and in many cases the student has friends who will witness that the teacher provoked the fight. Very few public school students have the courage to defend the teacher's rights, and an innocent teacher will be professionally harmed by the incident because in many instances he will be considered a bully who has picked on a smaller student.

Students are threatened daily. Physical assaults (as subtle as a bump) can harm students so emotionally that they will not attend school or even board a bus. Board of education members do not realize the bitterness that ensues because students are required to ride a school bus daily. Many students can cope with the problems, but it must be understood that a school bus driver is hardly able to drive a bus safely and also protect those students who are being physically and verbally abused. Can you imagine a teacher facing the blackboard and trying to control fifty students for the next half-hour?

There are no certification courses to assist a teacher in coping with violence. The rumors that circulate most frequently and are accepted by teachers are that boards of education prefer teachers to live with the problems because students and parents are apt to obtain the services of a lawyer.

Even though individual members of boards of education are aware of many discipline problems in the schools, these people in most instances ignore the problem or in some circumstances require the administrators and teachers to crack down on the most serious violations. Fighting, drug abuse, and vandalism now merit some attention, but the classroom disturbances continue because the teachers, administrators, and boards of education are somewhat proud and content with the limited step that they have employed to curtail what they consider to be the most serious violations.

Whenever violence occurs in the hallways or on school property, there is a problem that must be corrected, and the board of education that is satisfied because a few suspensions have been assigned is certainly gullible and naive. Fights among large numbers of students do not occur unless there is a reason. The reason may be deep-seated or it may be an immediate reaction to what a couple of students have done to offend other students.

An unintelligent school board actually complimented administration for suspending a few students when they should have insisted on knowing all the steps that had been taken toward eliminating future problems. A capable administration would have talked to all of the students involved, and, if there had been any respect for that administration, the truth would have been discovered. The truth was that a few students were grabbing girls' posteriors and making crude four-letter-word suggestions. The boyfriends and their friends believed that they were justified in reacting physically to rectify that repulsive behavior. The administration made no effort to change the attitudes of all of these students by being fair and firm with them, and this group of students caused problems for other school personnel as they continued through the school system. They continue to harbor hostility, even as adults.

3

If the students had had respect for the fairness of the administration, they would have complained that other students were molesting their girlfriends and would not have needed to fight in seeking justice. The ill-informed school board was led to wrong conclusions.

I have worked in public schools where girls threatened teachers and guidance counselors with knives, a girl challenged three boys to a fight, boys attacked teachers with combs and scissors, a boy hit a secretary, boys physically attempted to and sometimes did hurt teachers, girls challenged teachers to fight them, and teachers physically struck or manhandled students. Those school districts are fully endorsed by the evaluators for the Middle Atlantic states and are located in very good neighborhoods. Yes, there is violence even in the better school districts.

Violence is treated within the schools as it would be handled on the outside. When laymen insist on tough measures, the violence will be eliminated, the teachers will be able to teach, and the good students will be happier and able to learn more.

Nora Scott Kinzer, in her book *Stress and the American Woman*, stated:

> Aggression, however, is learned behavior, not necessarily triggered by a special male hormone. Little girls are taught to be clean and tidy and not fight. Mothers tolerate dirty little boys and fathers encourage their sons to "beat the crap out of any bully who starts a fight with you." Thus a tomboy is a physically aggressive little girl who plays boys' games, beats up on her boy playmate, and generally doesn't act like a nice little girl. *

---

*Nora Scott Kinzer, *Stress and the American Woman* (Garden City, N.Y.: Anchor Press/Doubleday, 1979), p. 12.

Many parents of children in the public schools have instructed their offspring to retaliate physically to contact or mere words. Many years ago it was relatively safe to respond physically because society accepted the responses as manly and somewhat civilized, but parents who insist on this today are subjecting their children to attacks from knives, combs, chains, belt buckles, and gangs of hoodlums. Administrators should be brave and intelligent enough to suspend those students who are annoying other students with physical actions and words; therefore, demanding parents are not being fair to their childen when they make them become part of the violence in the schools. If you or your children do not receive cooperation from the administration, you can replace those administrators.

DISRUPTIVE STUDENTS

Teachers have normally entered the profession because they have appreciated the teaching that they received and have the desire to emulate that instruction. Granted, some people have entered the profession for other reasons, but informal conversations reveal that most teachers entered education because they wanted to help others learn.

Courses offered by colleges equip the teacher with subject knowledge, teaching techniques, and, hopefully, confidence, but colleges have not been of much help in offering their students methods that enable them to work effectively with disruptive students.

It is recognized that schools have been unique in handling (or not handling) disruptive students. The school itself appears to modify the handling according to the board of education constituency, the superintendent, principal, assistant principal, teacher, or even the politics of the student involved! Consistency is not the mood of most discipline policies, at least in their enforcement.

6

What actually is a disruptive student? An impression generally held is that he/she might display emotion at times, but a more realistic impression is that a disruptive student does not want to be in school and will be disruptive at least some time each day if not during most classes. Some teachers are rather effective in restraining the behavior of these students, but it must be considered that even these teachers could help the other students much more if they did not have to give so much time and attention to the disruptive students.

Place yourself in the classroom. You have selected a short story for the students to read at home. You have prepared a vocabulary exercise. Your lesson plans are outstanding and your objectives for the lesson are appropriate. You believe that the students will certainly learn new information today, but will you be able to teach when John begins to annoy Betty? What will you do or say when John tells you that you're always picking on him? What will you do when Ray, Ted, and Mary agree with John? Will you send John to the office when you sense that (1) John will convince the administrator that you picked on him today; (2) the administrator will remember that you are sending him problems that he told you to handle; or (3) the administrator will give John a detention or internal suspension? When assigned to internal suspension the student is detained in a room with other students who have broken school rules. He does not attend his regularly assigned classes. The student will be returned to your classroom and probably will be disruptive again. Now, what do you do, especially when item 2 above is an important part of most administrators' philosophies?

Some teachers possess superior knowledge, an experience background that can vicariously serve the needs of the students, and an enthusiasm concerning education that would be contagious for most students, but the disruptive student is determined that he/she will be the central person in the classroom. An administrator who is not astute, and many are not, will not see the potential residing in this person and will do nothing to stop the antics of the student who is depriving all other students in the classroom of wonderful educational experiences. Administrators focus on a teacher's weakness and ignore the problem, which is the disruptive student.

Teachers have been exposed to so many disturbances that they become immune and actually believe that the disturbances are meant to be tolerated; with such an attitude there will be no improvement but more chaos. The better students eventually follow the example because they see no form of correction extended by the teacher. The problem exists because administrators have ignored the problem and accepted less worthy priorities.

Emotionally disturbed students are placed in the public schools today, and teachers who have problems in attempting to educate the regular public school students now have to contend with students who in many instances are incapable of learning in a normal classroom environment.

The students whom you see annoying others at the beach, ignoring lifeguards, stealing pocketbooks, running you off the road in their cars, mugging defenseless women and men, using armed robbery, and killing prison guards are the same students who attend public schools.

Some of these students are very street-wise, and many school employees choose to turn their heads in another direction rather than face physical assault or property damage. Many school employees will not live in the school community where they are employed.

A disruptive student will move from one seat to another seat, tap his foot or pen, mumble or whistle, sharpen his pencil, kick or hit other students sitting near him, throw paper clips or spit balls, call aloud whenever he desires, and steal anything he can. These inconsiderate disruptions will continue unless the teachers and administrators correct the violators or remove them from the classrooms.

STUDENT DISCIPLINE GUIDE

The board of education is responsible for adopting a student discipline guide that will permit the teacher to instruct without interruption. The board of education is also responsible for insuring its implementation.

Certain boards of education have used administrators, teachers, students, parents, and other citizens to establish a workable and fair guide.

A superior guide will list the violations and the discipline to be assigned to violators for breaking these rules. School boards must categorize violations into levels of serious and less serious offenses so that students can more easily grasp the seriousness of the violations.

Level I offenses could be minor offenses such as arriving late to school or homeroom. The teacher or administrative action would probably be to assign a detention. Level II offenses could be more serious violations:

1. Cutting class
2. Smoking (possibly in unauthorized areas)

3. Leaving school without permission
4. Truancy
5. Bus disturbances
6. Insubordination
7. Verbal assault
8. Willful fighting
9. Other serious offense (reckless driving, etc.)

For the above offenses the West Chester Area School District, Pennsylvania, has assigned administrative action which has tremendously improved the discipline at the secondary school level.

The steps are as follows:

1. A first offense will result in a one-school-day internal suspension.
2. A second offense will result in a three-school-day internal suspension.
3. A third offense will result in a five-school-day internal suspension.
4. A fourth offense will result in another five-school-day internal suspension. (This is the final in-school suspension.)
5. A fifth offense will result in a five-school-day external suspension.
6. A sixth offense will result in a ten-school-day external suspension.
7. A seventh offense will result in another ten-school-day external suspension from school with an administrative recommendation for expulsion.

The student has received guidance from administrators, guidance counselor, case worker, and other suitable personnel. Parent conferences have also been held.

11

Level III offenses are of such a nature that their commission represents a violation of law.

1. Theft
2. Physical assault
3. Possessing deadly weapon
4. Destruction of school property
5. Arson or false alarms
6. Bomb threats
7. Vandalism
8. Controlled substance abuse (drugs or alcohol)
9. Extortion

For Level III violations a first offense will result in a ten-school-day external suspension. For the second offense another ten-school-day external suspension from school will result, and the administration will recommend expulsion.

In this school district of approximately 5,150 secondary students, only fourteen students were referred to the board of education for expulsion. Students need guidelines and will respond to authority whenever they want to remain in school. The students who were expelled in most cases did not want to remain in school, and the administrators working to change the attitudes of these students learned that the students were determined to get out of school one way or another. When the students were expelled from schools, there was much less peer pressure on other students to cut classes, roam halls, or be truant.

Although the above guide has brought about a great improvement in disciplining students for those offenses, if a school district is to remove much of the stress brought about because of student disruptions, then the board of education must place an emphasis on the immediate classroom environment and the curbing of student disturbances which negate the teaching and learning that should have priority.

The teacher must be assured that no interruptions will be tolerated and that the disruptive students will be disciplined and also removed from the classroom should the behavior persist. Students who are disruptive throughout the school should be disciplined as serious offenders, and the repeat classroom disturber should also be treated as a serious offender.

There are no magic numbers in establishing a discipline guide, but one thing is definite: the students must understand that they will be expelled from school whenever those limits have been reached. Students are entitled to have a formal hearing before a board committee which will give the students another opportunity to prove that they are innocent. They might also ask to be placed on probation. The law requires a formal hearing and a competent board of education will provide an honest hearing.

School districts have expelled students for committing only one drug or alcohol abuse violation. Other school districts suspend students for a thirty-day period. For smoking cigarettes some school districts fine the students fifteen or thirty-five dollars and also suspend them for a few days. Boards of education have much discretion in establishing discipline codes, and wise school board members will seek ideas and cooperation from administrators, teachers, students, and laymen.

Children will tell parents that all of the kids smoke marijuana and drink alcohol. The construction of the building and the surrounding properties can make it easy or difficult for the administrators in curbing these illegal practices. Students are in classes except for a thirty-minute lunch period and the three or five minutes that they need

13

to pass from one classroom area to another. If the students are supervised during lunch period, the only opportunities they have to smoke are before they get on the school buses in the morning or after they leave the school in the afternoon. Marijuana has a distinctive odor, which teachers and administrators can readily detect, so I do not believe that your children are telling you the truth when they say that everyone is smoking, especially in the schools. Very few students are able to find a few minutes where they have the privacy to smoke while they are in school. Students who drive cars to school have more privacy and obviously do more smoking if this is their intention.

Another exaggerated statement is that the best students always smoke marijuana. Having served as a coordinator to eliminate drug and alcohol abuse, I was able to communicate and relate with students on a personal and friendly basis. They would confide in me because they realized that I was really concerned with their welfare, and, even though I strongly disagreed with their beliefs, all of our conversations were to be private.

In researching the levels of academic accomplishments among the 110 students in a high school of 1,860, these students who used marijuana regularly achieved the following marks: A's — 3; B's — 42; C's — 121; D's — 150; F's — 196.

Students earning the A's and B's did this in social studies and English courses where they were able to verbalize with street language, but these students were not able to do well in the sciences, mathematics, and foreign language areas where more structured learning was required. The information I obtained is more accurate than that obtained through surveys or by someone not working directly with the students using the marijuana.

In the 1960s the Canadian Psychiatric Association

14

stated that marijuana has a lasting impression on its users which results in psychotic and unusual social behavior. The National Institute of Mental Health reported that regular use of marijuana contributes to characteristic personality changes — apathy, loss of effectiveness, and diminished capacity or willingness to carry out complex long-term plans, endure frustration, concentrate for long periods, follow routines, or successfully master new material.

The latest research in 1980 substantiates the earlier reports. Marijuana:

- can hurt your heart and your lungs;
- can impair your coordination and vision as you drive a car, motorcycle, or any vehicle;
- can hinder your thinking and conversations;
- can stay in your body for a week;
- can cause cancer;
- is stronger than cigarettes. Smoking five marijuana cigarettes a week can do more harm to your lungs than smoking six packs of regular cigarettes;
- can raise heart rate by as much as 50 percent;
- can affect the hormones;
- can give abnormal sperm and lower the level of testosterone;
- can be contaminated by the "pushers."

Elementary, intermediate, and secondary students are developing from childhood into manhood and womanhood. Wise, responsible parents will always be conscious of the behavior patterns exhibited by their children. When children defend the practices of abuse or their friends who engage in these practices, you should check to see how your children are spending their allowances or what type of junk they are hiding in their pocketbooks and closets. I do believe that the health of your children is more important to you than some unreasonable guilt you might have because you are intruding on your children's right to privacy.

Although it might be difficult for you to understand why school personnel will not inform you that your children are always with children who have a reputation for using drugs and alcohol, it is because some parents have acted irrationally. Parents repeat to other parents and neighborhood children what an administrator has told them in confidence, and then that administrator is unable to help other students in the school because the students believe that the administrator cannot be trusted with their problems.

School districts can use other steps. School district personnel:

- must do everything within their power to provide supervision so that all parents will be assured that their children will not be offered the opportunity to use drugs during the school day;
- have the responsibility to furnish the latest drug knowledge for your youngsters. Fear, arrests, force, facts, guidance, and all the approaches that are used, in many instances, do not overcome the youth's desire for thrills, peer acceptance, dares, confrontations, recognition, and identity;
- should remind parents to show mature understanding by building an honest rela-

tionship with their children. You will not be conned (deceived) if you concern yourself with the *study habits* of your youngsters and concern yourself less with their friends. You should have enough love and trust among your sons and daughters that you always know where they are. Even though this doesn't guarantee you that they won't make mistakes, at least you have a good relationship and a support to begin anew whenever it is necessary. You must be firm when you are right (are you positive?), but do not take a stand when your reasons can be challenged. Do not make a rule unless it's necessary to protect someone. Don't come down too hard on hair styles, but you must discipline rebellious children.

Since many measures to correct drug and alcohol abuse are pushed aside by stronger youth drives, strive early to develop strong academic, athletic, church, and community interests. Ask your son or daughter to observe those students who are involved in the drug scene. Are these students "making it"? Are they competing successfully? What kind of home life do you envision for them when they graduate? My observation is, not all, but most of them better develop different study habits if they intend to compete and rear a family. Most students eventually learn that drug abuse must end, but steps must be taken to minimize the damage that will linger long after the students have given up the harmful abuses.

VANDALISM AND THEFT

Rebellious students break windows, paneling, stalls, doors, laboratory equipment, etc. Automobiles and motorbikes can be run back and forth over school property until the turf becomes uprooted. Seven-hundred-dollar typewriters and movie projectors disappear. There is usually more vandalism in a school when students become upset at administration rules and acts, or whenever they wish to make life miserable for a teacher.

Students are causing extensive damage by dropping fireworks in toilets. They frighten and also cause injury when they throw fireworks among unsuspecting groups of students. Certain activities are definitely associated with graduation-type pranks, but, even then, more destructive pranks occur whenever the students believe that they can perform these destructive pranks with more general peer approval. Movie and television martial arts products are more frequently imitated today, and the students are pleased that they can break windows with a well-aimed kick or hand blow. Fires occur more frequently, as a few students delight in igniting rolls of toilet paper or hand towels or in throwing matches or cigarette butts into trash cans. School boards must publicize a protective policy that will remove these violators from the school.

A very important objective that professors fail to mention to students is that the teachers must be careful in guarding personal possessions such as pocketbooks, wallets, and books. Students are capable of stealing these objects during the five or ten seconds that the student teacher or teacher is occupied elsewhere. Teachers become very much attached to the students and do not believe that the children would ever stoop so low. Permissive psychologists would probably defend the students and blame the stealings on the teachers because the adults were careless and the children could not avoid such great temptations.

Acts of vandalism and theft are pressures that teachers must contend with and it does not take much imagination to realize how disturbing these student actions can be to a teacher who has tried to be fair and helpful.

Some acts of vandalism are more of a nuisance to the school district because, even though the damage does not disturb the educational program, the taxpayer will be contributing $25,000 to repair and replace school property. The money should be used for purchasing educational materials, not for maintenance.

Acts of vandalism that are much more painful to teachers and students occur whenever disruptive students steal or destroy materials that the teachers need to make the lesson more interesting. Lack of materials brings about a revision in the learning environment and undoubtedly diverts from the objectives previously planned by teachers. The methods and materials to be used in obtaining objectives have been influenced, if not dictated, by disruptive students!

19

Parents should remind students to wear practical jackets to school rather than more expensive ones. Some students carelessly allow other students to learn their locker combination numbers, and, when this occurs, clothing, books, lunches, and other personal items are stolen. Other students are negligent in carrying a lot of money to school. The administration should be happy to guard a large sum for students, especially for those students selling materials for a school money-making project. Remind your childen that under no circumstances should they expose money or leave a pocketbook unattended.

Public school administrators must take steps to minimize the amount of vandalism and theft that is taking place in the school district. Employees in maintenance and custodial positions must be screened carefully before they are employed. These people receive very little supervision on the job, and most stealing of expensive typewriters, movie projectors, speaking systems, and other audio-visual equipment occurs after the general school personnel have left the premises and the custodians are the only personnel in the building. Some school systems have invested in sound-alarm systems to apprehend the people who are stealing. To finance this type of system in all schools is most expensive. If you decide to employ night watchmen to make visits to the schools being vandalized and burglarized, you probably are as effective in minimizing the losses, but you would not be as effective in prosecuting the vandalizers, thieves, and intruders.

Teaching and administrative employees must assume the initial responsibility for protecting particular areas of school property during their working day, and it is the responsibility of the Board of Education to provide policies and supervisory personnel or systems that are able to secure the buildings during after-school and evening hours.

The board of education is responsible for providing the school district with facilities that can be used for extracurricular activities. The facilities should be isolated or in an area that can be blocked off from the regular curriculum areas at the close of the normal school day. Much vandalism occurs whenever the main building area is not separated from the gymnasium, cafeteria, or auditorium area.

Every school employee should be given responsibility for some area of security because it is most impractical to expect a few administrators and custodians to provide sufficient security. Custodians who are cleaning the building are not security men when they are cleaning classrooms and hallways, but they could use some of their work time for checking other areas of the school building.

Inventories must be designated for all employees, and these should be collated by supervisory and administrative personnel semi-annually if security is to receive proper evaluation and if the academic, athletic, and other extracurricular departments are to submit realistic budgets. Employees will be less likely to steal whenever the school district uses the proper inventory procedures and has sufficient personnel responsible for requisitioned supplies and equipment.

DEMANDING PARENTS

Many parents assume an aggressive role whenever they feel that their child is not receiving the best attention or whenever their child complains. Some parents profit from this aggressiveness, but at times there is a negative return. Yes, some teachers and administrators do not want any type of interference, especially from the students and their parents.

Whenever a parent is led to understand that a high IQ entitles his off-spring to an individualized form of instruction, the parent will normally follow through until there is satisfaction. Sometimes the parents take their concerns to the state departments of education, where they can usually find someone interested in a crusade. The educators recognize that some lawyer or pseudo-intellectual in a state office has decided that he will be more popular by insisting that these so-called brighter students get a stylized brand of education through grades K-12. The educators also realize that there is no reasonable explanation for spending more money to educate those students

22

who have a sometimes identifiable talent such as creativity, and yet the mainstream parents remain inactive in trying to give the majority of students a similar type of educational development.

Men and women are outstanding in business, education, government, and other areas, but they had no distinguishing talents during their school years and would not have been eligible to receive the individualized instruction that is forced on the public schools by a few very concerned people.

The forms of individualized programs for these students have not been successful; otherwise I would suggest that the silent majority campaign for similar programs. Having observed most types of instruction through classroom evaluations, observations, and visitations, I am one-hundred-percent positive that the teacher who is knowledgeable and stimulating, modifies teaching techniques, and allows students to interact through various discussion and writing activities is the teacher who is providing the best and most practical types of education for all students.

Reticent and other less-sophisticated parents will not visit schools because they find that they are unable to cope with the overwhelming number of people at a conference. Some teachers will schedule a person-to-person conference, which most parents can handle; however, today, a parent upon walking into a school is confronted by an administrator, counselor, caseworkers, and a team of four or five teachers. On the surface it appears that the school is really concerned, but in most instances a student's problem is with one teacher, and that teacher, parent, and student should be the three people who can best solve that problem. A parent can then confer with an administrator if there is no improvement.

Teachers forget that many parents are nervous concerning any contact with a teacher, and any form of intimidation will be resented. A parent should certainly be offered the opportunity to choose the type of conference that he/she can handle without unnecessary stress.

Parents frequently expect their children to succeed in learning situations that are too difficult or not interesting for them. For example, parents force students to take a foreign language when the students have no interest in a foreign language. The students will not be able to learn a language successfully when foreign language teachers are required to have the students reach standards that are beyond the abilities of these students. The foreign language curriculum should embrace opportunities for all students to learn a language of their choice and if necessary at a much slower pace than those presently used in intermediate and secondary schools. Well-intentioned parents should exert enough pressure so that school board members will understand that well-educated students need to be exposed to a foreign language or to the fundamentals of many languages if they are to be educated properly. Many students are able to learn a foreign language at the pace presently being used, but the better schools will realize the value of giving a superior education to all students.

Domineering parents frequently put unneeded stress on their children to take courses that are academically too difficult for them. The children as a result of this stress will tell lies, grow more nervous, and generally live in an unreal world! High school students will have a very difficult time in obtaining an "A" when they are taking difficult subjects, and even more often they will find it hard to get good grades whenever they are enrolled in classes where the teacher has excessively high standards. Many students have complained to me about the problems that they encounter in their homes from dissatisfied parents.

Parents who form or join school booster clubs can control activities unless the coaches, administrators, band directors, etc. are aware of this unwarranted aggression. Members of booster organizations have been able to decide student award winners and have used their strength to criticize and oust coaches. Athletic teams have been weakened when coaches have submitted to parental pressures. Often the coaches have been pressured by administrators who were persuaded by the parents. Parents have every right to pressure educators in all areas of curriculum in efforts to improve the educational objectives, but public school personnel must not let the public dictate to the coaches or teachers which students should be playing and which students should be receiving awards for their performances. When you come right down to it, why should the schools or parents declare any students to be most valuable, best athletes, best musicians, etc.? We know that it is used for public relations, but is it good public relations and is it worthwhile?

The demanding parents who belong to PTAs for the purpose of improving instruction, enlarging the curriculum, and supporting student activities are the parents that the school districts really need. The demanding parents who are determined to support their own children regardless of right or wrong are the parents who have offended many teachers and as a result made cooperation sometimes very hard to obtain.

FEAR, INSECURITY, AND PRESSURE

Teachers in some school districts are very well protected by local, state, and national associations and unions. This protection was probably brought into existence when board of education members and administrators were firing employees because some important taxpayer did not like the employee, a local person wanted a teaching job, etc.

Tenure supposedly protects an employee's job, but, in reality, this is not true. Even though the law spells out that there are only a few legitimate reasons for firing an employee, a school district can contend that there is a drop in enrollment or a needed curriculum change. The department of education will give approval even though there is no proof that the curriculum change will improve the educational environment.

No one in the public schools can guarantee teachers that a board of education or a personnel director will be competent in projecting the needs of the school district. A teacher is hired under the pretense that the school district is in a rapidly growing community and that this is certainly the place if he/she is looking for advancement or for wonderful working conditions. Within a year or two the teacher is looking for another job because some incompetent people hired too many employees.

Even when the teacher is not dropped, the insecurity of working under such dreadful circumstances affects the morale of all professionals because they are being subjected to the whims of an administrator who has the power to change the educational program every year. For example, an administrator can decide that he needs three art teachers this year instead of two. Another teacher must be dropped. Will he/she decide to drop an English, math, science, reading, physical education teacher, or a guidance counselor? What if he/she decided to hire two teaching aides in place of a teacher? Which department will lose a teacher?

Imagine that you are working in an office and the boss decides that every year he'll need to make a change. Would you enjoy working under this condition?

Suppose that you are one of three guidance counselors. You are new in the school as a counselor even though you have had twenty years of successful teaching. A much younger counselor receives a higher evaluation than you because he/she had evidently "pushed a pencil" for her evaluator on a number of occasions, and the evaluator personally feels that this is more important than counseling students, working with parents, and supporting teachers. A hard-nosed person would suggest that you look for another job, even though he should be smart enough to realize that any move you make will cost you at least three thousand dollars, assuming you were lucky enough to get another job.

The more logical and humane way would be for the Board of Education, which establishes policy, to devise an evaluation form insuring that the important components of an employee's work are measured objectively with supporting data. This has not been accomplished in an honest and fair manner; therefore, the teachers have fought for seniority.

Dr. Ralph G. Hirshowitz, M.D., an Associate of the Levinson Institute and Assistant Clinical Professor of Psychiatry at Harvard Medical School, has done a considerable amount of research on stress. Interesting comments are the following:

> Of 2,800 businessmen in a recent survey, almost 30 percent reported job-related health problems and that this percentage will continue to rise . . . Stress in itself is neither good or bad. Some people master stressful situations and other people deteriorate in emotional and physical health . . . An organization can create a supportive atmosphere to ease that strain so that a stressful situation can be a creative learning experience.*

Teachers are not the only people in the public schools being placed in an unnecessarily stressful environment. Students are also being placed in situations of unneeded stress. They are hesitant to complain to teachers because many teachers will not correct the abuse source that is annoying students; some teachers will not handle the problem discreetly, and some teachers don't want to hear about the abuses. Students hesitate to report problems brought about by incompetent teachers because usually they don't know the administrators, nor do they have

---

*"Addendum" — a special feature of "The Levinson Letter." Remarks were reported by Jacqui Bishop in *Management Practice*, the newsletter of Coloney, Canon, Maine and Purcell, Inc., Copyright, 1973.

confidence in their methods.

Some teachers and students can reflect on the Twenty-third Psalm or John 3:16 to subdue the stresses that threaten their physical, mental, and emotional welfare, but other educators and students need to see evidence of strong supportive measures from the board of education if they are to be helped in avoiding physical, mental, or emotional breakdowns.

James A. Michener during an interview was asked, "What worries you? About what are you pessimistic?" In response to the questions posed by Bill Stall of the *Los Angeles Times Service*, Michener responded,

> To see the deterioration of the public schools is just shocking. And since I am a total product of public education, I have a sort of vested interest in this. The fact is that many classrooms are arenas in which purposeful learning can't take place. The incompetence of teachers. Lack of discipline. The failure of society to support education. All of these are very worrisome.
>
> Some of it stems from that damn Vietnam War in which we allowed young men to avoid the draft if they stayed in teaching. *

---

* *The Philadelphia Inquirer, Philadelphia, Pa., July 22, 1979.*

INADEQUATE SALARIES

Local, state, and national organizations have been supportive in teachers' attempts to keep abreast of inflation. Agreed, it is most difficult to place a dollar value on the teaching and related school performances of an individual teacher, especially when the tax structure differs markedly from one school district to another. Another problem is to decide the amount of money to pay your administrators and supervisors. Boards of education must first select more practical objectives by which to rate them.

Administrators who are considered to be more capable by teachers, students, parents, and counselors should certainly be rated superior by all evaluation systems. Boards of education that are to establish policy should certainly be capable of setting up objective procedures. Personal friendship awards should be replaced by awards to whoever is really doing a good job!

Teacher observations have very little objectivity as they are implemented in schools. A teacher will normally teach five periods each day for 180 school days. Although the teacher instructs classes for 900 different periods, she is observed during two of those class periods!

Even though a school does not normally award merit increases because it is recognized that it is not fair under present observation techniques, employees are dismissed from their positions because some supervisor or administrator subjectively makes a decision. This unfair decision can drastically change that teacher's life.

Administrators and supervisors have someone in line for at least 95 percent of all job openings. The hypocrisy begins with the hiring and does not end with the firing, but begins all over again.

Knowing what supervisors and administrators do, I am constantly amazed by the decisions that are made by members of boards of education when they pay some supervisors and administrators $10,000 and $15,000 more than they pay the top-paid teacher. Will some board member please step forward and let us know what remarkable mental decisions are being made by the giants in education?

Teachers in the school are the employees who work with the students in the classroom. Teachers in any good school district are doing what little curriculum revision needs to be accomplished, and they are the ones who must continue to learn the curriculum changes which may or may not be useful for elementary, middle, or secondary students.

The administrator's major job is to help maintain discipline so that the teachers can teach. Yes, administrators and supervisors should be in classrooms to suggest ways in which teachers can improve instruction.

The suggestion is that administrators would be paid for extra time that they should extend in attending and supervising after-school and evening activities. Maybe

31

combat time, too, because some administrators must placate irate and violent students.

Ten to fifteen thousand dollars — whew!

A school district should award merit increases to administrative and supervisory personnel only after establishing guidelines that rate an employee in all areas of his assignments and take into consideration his relationships with the people he is in direct contact with on a regular basis. The relationship that an administrator or supervisor has with the students and all school employees is most important in any evaluation because mutual respect will generate the most conducive student learning environment.

Good administrators need a year on the job to understand what the strengths and weaknesses really are, but I cannot believe that anyone would need more time than a summer preceding the second year to institute the important changes that must be made.

Most decisions that administrators make should require little discretion because a good school district will have policies that must be followed, and these should certainly provide the actions to be taken in major areas. A major fault of most school districts is that they do not provide proper policies, and the administrative decisions will often be inconsistent. For example, a high school principal walked into a boys' lavatory and suspended all of the students because someone had been smoking! Teachers and administrators frequently punished an entire class when one or two students were disruptive. Should students who sneak out of a study hall five minutes early be suspended or given detention? School district policies must provide for proper actions by administrators; therefore, an administrator is basically supervising and administering in line with established policies.

32

A principal has assistants, counselors, and a teaching staff to help make major decisions. I am not attempting to minimize the hard work that some principals do, but I am endeavoring to show that the more difficult work connected with administration is not in making decisions that remarkably alter the education programs. Instead, there is more pressure in working with kids "high on drugs," with students who have chips on their shoulders, and in breaking up and preventing fights. Some teachers are also hard to work with.

A good administrator will:

- attend, supervise, and sometimes assist at high school athletic contests (football, basketball, wrestling, volleyball, tennis, soccer, cross country, field hockey, baseball, track and field, gymnastics, etc.) as well as support junior varsity and freshman sports;

- attend and supervise school dances, proms, fashion shows, drama shows, band and choral concerts, PTA special events, etc.

Administrators are responsible for student behavior at extracurricular programs. Yes, administrators should be paid more because of the stresses and pressures associated with the job and for the enormous amount of time necessary to supervise extracurricular activities. Most administrative decisions require good common sense, not textbook interpretations.

EVALUATIONS

Subjective is the word most commonly used to describe the form of evaluation that has been used in determining the value of the work performance done daily by teachers, supervisors, and administrators.

Evaluations have been based on philosophies of the leaders in education, on psychological viewpoints, on personality traits associated with good leaders, on teaching behavior, on competency-based approaches, and on numerous other approaches.

Even though the evaluation systems strongly state that their primary purpose is to improve instruction, there is little emphasis on this purpose whenever a rating of outstanding, very good, good, satisfactory, or unsatisfactory is marked on the observation form. Instead, the statements enumerating strengths, weaknesses, and suggestions should be emphasized.

Students have an opportunity to write the correct answers to questions and mathematically awarded a 75, 80, or a similar rating, but teachers are not answering questions, and under the present forms of evaluation only a most unsophisticated judge, administrator, supervisor, or board of education can believe that an evaluator is capable of objectively rating a teacher, supervisor, or administrator.

The evaluator's comments which list the weaknesses and recommendations for improvement are certainly much more defensible than an arbitrary rating by an evaluator. Four administrators and a supervisor can easily arrive at five different ratings for the same teacher during an observation period.

Although I do not believe that evaluators can arrive at any degree of objectivity with five categories, I do believe that we can use three categories and with proper guidelines can make most observation periods objective enough to improve instruction and to defend our impression of the teaching performance during the period of observation.

In any successful evaluation system the evaluator must be prepared to observe the teacher for at least six periods over a two- or three-day period.

A teacher must be observed for preparation, teaching techniques, and student reaction. The teacher should be rated outstanding, good, or unsatisfactory in each area.

The observation form that will most nearly approach complete objectivity follows:

O G U

Comments:

I. Preparation
  A. Written lesson plans_____
    Grade Book_____
  B. Objectives stated
    1. Clarity of objectives
    2. Appropriate for class
  C. Audio-visual aids and other
    material

The observer must understand the teacher's objectives for the students. Does he have any? Too much credit is given for how well a teacher lectures.

D. Organization (activities,
   chores)
E. Provides for learning new
   material
II. Teaching Techniques
   A. Follows written lesson plans
   B. Activities implement stated
      objectives
   C. Teaching pace
   D. Lecture
      Discussion
      Question-probing
      Audio
      Visual
      Textbook____Worksheet____
      Oral Reading
      Oral Response
      (Individual____Unison____)
      Large Group
      Small Group
      Individualized
      Provides for evaluation
      Homework
III. Student Reaction
   A. Participation
      Total_____
      Partial_____
      Passive_____
   B. Enthusiasm
   C. Critical thinking opportunities
   D. Rapport

Don't rate the teacher; rate the teaching-learning environment. The teacher is responsible for written plans, objectives, approaches, techniques, content, motivation, evaluation, and student reaction, not just the lecture that he gives.

Other personnel must be evaluated according to the needs for their existence. A superintendent is evaluated by the following:

O G U

I. Programs Submitted to Board for
   Board Decision
   A. Educational program
   B. Financial program
   C. Educational supportive
      services

Comments:
The superintendent must be intelligent and confident enough to select subordinates who have strengths that the school district lacks.

36

D. Community relationships

II. Educational Leadership
Evaluated by
A. Central office staff
B. Administrative and supervisory staff
C. Teaching staff
D. Supportive staff
E. Community organizations and individuals
F. Parents and students

The superintendent's priority should be loyal personnel. I have worked with superintendents whose subordinates laughed at the decisions and personalities of their boss. Even though a boss has weaknesses, no professional has a right to tear down a school district or any individual through vicious comments.

All assistants reporting directly to the superintendent are to be evaluated by him in the following areas:

O G U

I. Assignments
A. Supported board of education policies
B. Work assigned by superintendent
C. Work dictated by job description
D. Additional assignments
E. Volunteered efforts

II. Relationships with
A. Superintendent
B. Central office personnel
C. Administrators and supervisor
D. Teaching staff
E. Supportive staff
F. Individuals and community organizations
G. Parents and students

Comments:
School districts must hire only those assistants who are involved in public school educational programs.

Supervisors can be hired to direct maintenance, transportation, buildings and grounds, adult education, etc.

A wise school board will hire one or two supervisors to closely and frequently observe those teachers who are not doing a good job. These supervisors whenever they are supported by the board can be more objective in working to improve the techniques of the weaker teachers. Supervisory positions should be considered a responsibility, not a reward.

Principals and assistant principals are to be evaluated according to similar procedures.

O G U

I. Assignments
   A. Supported board of education policies
   B. Work assigned by superior (transportation, scheduling, etc.)
   C. Work dictated by job description (discipline, attendance, etc.)
   D. Additional assignments (cafeteria, assemblies, MBOs, etc.)
   E. Volunteered efforts (concerts, athletic activities, community groups, etc.)

II. Relationships with
   A. Superior
   B. Central office personnel
   C. Teaching staff
   D. Supportive staff
   E. Community organizations
   F. Parents
   G. Students

Scheduling, discipline, improving instruction, and student activities are the major responsibilities.

Principals must treat all subordinates equally.

Unless opinions are selected from a large number of people, there is no objectivity to an evaluation. I repeat, a large number of people must evaluate.

The principal is mainly responsible for the instructional program. The assistant principal must be evaluated for the discipline in all areas of the school building. The supervisor must be primarily concerned with teaching techniques. All other duties are subordinate for these educators.

An area that is completely neglected in giving a more accurate measurement of teaching qualities is the success of the students in mastering the subject content. There are teachers who appear to be doing a good job in using teaching techniques during the observed teaching period, but there is not the same enthusiasm for the teaching performance when at the end of the year very many students have failed the final exam, dropped considerably in marks supposedly earned, and are among numerous failures for the year.

The board of education should adopt a policy requiring each teacher in the school district to submit a mark tabulation indicating the number of As, Bs, Cs, Ds, and Fs earned by students. Is a teacher an outstanding one when 40 out of the 120 students fail the course? Either the teacher's tests are too difficult, the standards are too high, or the teacher is unsatisfactory and must receive better supervision. Why hasn't the board of education directed the administration to correct those situations so that the students would receive a better education and a greater opportunity to achieve success?

Your board of education has the responsibility of evaluating all areas of the educational program. Evaluation for the purpose of improving the education program will list the weaknesses and strengths of all areas. Recommendations should certainly be made by the evaluators, and the board of education must assign responsibility for seeing that the desired recommendations are implemented.

Teachers and administrators must support an objective evaluation system, but there is no justification for placing individuals in five categories implying that they are outstanding (an "A" employee), very good (a "B" employee), good (a "C" employee), satisfactory (a "D" employee), or unsatisfactory (an "E" employee). What boards of education indicate is that an evaluator can observe a class and truthfully say that a teacher almost did a very good job during the period but not quite; therefore, he/she will receive a good rating? On many days a teacher is totally prepared, the objectives are great, but the students are not all really interested in giving their best. If you have ever taught, you realize that some days when you have not been as well prepared, the lessons are outstanding because all of the students came to learn! It is not fair to classify a teacher as "B" or "C" when there are factors beyond the control of the teacher. It is much more honest to say that the teacher did a good job. The evaluator can defend his/her evaluation because he realizes that the lesson was not unsatisfactory nor was it outstanding. The evaluator and the teacher are now in a better mood to improve instruction when they discuss motivational techniques.

ORGANIZATION AND FUNCTIONS

School board members are exposed to many operations during their period of service. A good school board member will require administrators to submit three or four practical solutions to the board so that they can make intelligent decisions. If rubber stamping is to be avoided, board of education members must be provided with workable alternatives in addition to the policy that the administration prefers. It is very easy to sell a vanilla ice cream cone, but it must be recognized that some people prefer chocolate or Neapolitan.

The internal organization of the board is important. In no circumstance should a board of education be allowed to handpick members when there are candidates who have campaigned successfully and are willing to serve.

The superintendent of schools will provide the agenda for meetings and enough information for a member to vote wisely. An attorney is also available to answer any questions demanding a legal interpretation. Board members only need common sense. The main point is that the

41

policies adopted by the board should cover all aspects of the education program, and, whenever there are problems, it is the responsibility of the board of education to make the corrections immediately.

As illogical as it seems there has been a case in which a board of education fired the business manager for a half-million-dollar mistake in the budget when anyone with any degree of intelligence must realize that the school budget is certainly one of the two most important responsibilities under any job description for the superintendent of schools. Politics, not common sense, was used in fixing the blame.

Policy drafting is normally the responsibility of the administration, and it is the most important responsibility of the board of education to adopt only those policies which appear to have immediate and long-range positive advantages for the students, parents, citizens, and employees of the school district. Refine what you have. Do not experiment with lives of students.

The organization of the employees should provide for clearly identified line and staff relationships. In many instances job descriptions are not at all indicative of the work performed by an employee. A supervisor of a particular department should have a written weekly schedule to follow which indicates to the immediate superior and board of education that the employee will be doing the work expected of a supervisor. If the schedule indicates that the employee is to sit behind a desk and do a lot of conversing on the telephone, then a different title should be assigned to the position, and the board of education should reassess the organization.

Although most boards of education permit the administration to do the hiring of employees (except for the head football coach!), my belief is that a less biased way of getting new ideas into an organization is for a committee of the board of education to interview administrators, supervisors, and teachers for vacancies that arise. If members of the board of education are really interested in using the talents that will improve the education program, they will find the time and opportunity to ask the candidates in what manner and in what areas they can improve the educational program.

Fiscal management responsibility does not apply only to the business manager's staff. Administrators and supervisors who are responsible for programs must be held accountable for all funds, and the board of education is responsible for seeing that some employee is assigned to oversee all spending. Money budgeted for some program cannot be switched to finance another project.

Organizations must insure that legal requirements are satisfied, bid specifications are complied with, and programs that need financing are not implemented unless it is proved that the programs can be part of a long-range goal. Bid specifications are frequently handled improperly. The lowest bidder is not awarded the contract even though he has comparable products. If you do not want any substitute, you must state this in the bid. Be sure that the business manager is able to invest money so that the taxpayers receive a good return on the bonds that are bought and sold.

Someone in the business office should be responsible for a yearly survey of bus transportation. All students living within the school district are to be provided a seat on the school bus, but the school district can insist that buses be assigned the maximum number of students and that the buses follow routes which will permit this. Administrators and bus owners in many school districts are intimate friends, and the public is the loser. If the board of education insists on fiscal responsibility, there will be more finances available to purchase educational materials for use by the classroom teacher.

You will agree that in a well-structured business organization an employee is responsible to one superior. In education very often a teacher must please a department head, a supervisor, an assistant principal (two or three), a principal, assistant superintendent, and even a superintendent! The best organization will provide one boss for an employee. Supportive staff should offer suggestions, teaching aids, and appropriate techniques but should not be in a line relationship.

CURRICULUM

Teachers before being certified to teach a subject are required to obtain a college degree that indicates that he/she has passed 120 or 130 undergraduate credits, depending on the requirements established by that college.

A majority of teachers continue to take graduate courses because it is necessary that they do so to be certified permanently and by obtaining thirty more credits they can acquire a master's degree. Additional credits do not indicate that they will be more knowledgeable than those teachers who do not obtain a master's degree, nor does it indicate that they will be better teachers.

It is unlikely that you or an experienced educator can observe a teaching performance and determine the type of degree possessed by a teacher. A college curriculum that provides a wide practical academic background in the liberal arts area would be more helpful to a graduate student who certainly should have ample knowledge in his teaching area since he has had at least thirty credits

45

(minimum of ten courses) while obtaining a major in the teaching area. The point is that teachers should be judged according to teaching performance and not pressured into taking courses because the board of education wants teachers to possess more degrees.

In-service programs are held to enhance a teacher professionally, but there is little evidence to indicate that these programs are worth the money involved. Administrations must plan the programs only after they have researched their schools' weaknesses and strengths. Programs need prior approval by teachers, and whenever possible, teachers should be given three or four choices to choose from because teachers' interests vary considerably. Evaluation following the program must indicate that the in-service was successful. Some are!

Curriculum clusters which are normally formed to solve problems in subject areas or in building relationships are helpful in curriculum development, but they are expensive when substitute teachers must cover classes.

Curriculum guides are available in all subject areas. Commercial companies have worked closely with educators in developing a curriculum at all grade levels. These programs are not expensive; however, the local school is very much conscious of implementing a curriculum that can be acclaimed for being unique. This can become a very expensive procedure, and, should a board of education decide that the students should be rated with other students on a state or national level, then the uniqueness of the local program will probably result in lower test scores on the national examination.

The curriculum should be articulated vertically from kindergarten through twelfth grade, but there is no reason why thousands of dollars should be spent in this attempt. Special care must be taken that the curriculum is not changed because a new supervisor is employed. For example, the English teachers might have agreed that certain paperback books are to be used at each grade level, and the supervisor autocratically states that an anthology is to be used at each grade level.

The new math emphasis of the 1950s is a good example of college professors deciding that the math curriculum had to be changed. Evaluating the programs as unsuccessful, the boards of education, state departments of education, and teachers realized that so much time had been used in endeavoring to teach the new math theories and techniques that insufficient time was being allotted for mastery of the fundamentals. As an evaluator of many math teaching performances it was implicit that the teachers had used a fifty-minute period to teach the same lesson that teachers in the 1930s and 1940s would have taught in five or ten minutes.

Teachers in most instances have taken at least fifteen courses in the subject area that they are teaching, and, because the vast majority of teachers understand subject content and are able to impart that content to the students when given the opportunity, efforts must be extended so that the opportunity to teach without interruptions is available.

Many schools experience bickering among staff departments and teachers because each department wishes to expand. Department members stress that:

- science needs aides to implement individualized instruction;
- computers be provided for new math programs;
- aides be hired to read and correct English compositions;
- field trip experiences be available to make use of local historical, governmental, and

other community resources;

- reading be individualized and a maximum of fifteen students be assigned for developmental reading and a maximum of eight students for remedial;
- elective coeducation courses be provided for most physical education activities.
- more selections be available for coeducational industrial arts and home economics classes.
- more health personnel be hired to meet the requirements for teaching additional courses in sex education and family living;
- the learning media center (library) needs audio-visual personnel and aides;
- foreign language laboratories need aides to protect the audio-visual equipment during the periods when teachers are not in the room;
- resource rooms be available for all major departments;
- business education have better communications in introducing students to the advantages of acquiring skills in typing, accounting, etc.
- advertising media such as photography, signs, designs, and crafts indicate that the art programs need to include more courses for development of special interests.
- the playing of musical instruments begin in the elementary schools and organized groups for band and chorus be taught during the regular school day.
- special education programs be provided for the social and emotional maladjusted

students, for the mentally retarded but educable students, for the physically handicapped students, and for the gifted students.

I'm waiting for someone to ask, "Which department areas are stressing the basics?!" Although no one really knows, I do believe that each teacher should rely on written objectives and that these objectives should indicate the important knowledge that will be taught by that teacher.

Revisions in the curriculum have been occurring in all subject areas because changes are inevitable, and the teachers should be knowledgeable about the curriculum that they must impart daily. Foreign language laboratories, English paperback books, and practical elective courses appear to be revisions that will become permanent.

Along with needed changes has come the jargon that has no immediate worth because it is foreign to the taxpayers. Educators are fascinated with "hands-on experiences," "think boxes," "anticipatory sets," "time on task," and countless other phrases. Football coaches have taken the lead in establishing a colorful nomenclature, and the press has given coaches favorable publicity for "red dogging," "nose guard," "blood end," "lonesome end," and hundreds of other catch phrases. The phrase that I find quite amusing was coined by a famous professional football coach in Texas. He refers to a "flexed end" or "flexed back." Actually his "flexed end" is moved out farther from the center of the main formation so he really is the "extended end," but who's going to challenge an expert in his field?! I must admit if you really don't give much thought to it, the phrase "flexed end" does sound good! If the educators' purpose is to communicate with the public, they are off course, but if the attempt is to develop a language that needs interpretation, they are on course.

The curriculum has been expanded so that elective courses supplement the basic courses offered in English, social studies, mathematics, science, foreign language, art, music, industrial arts, home economics, health, driver education, distributive education, business education, reading, work/study, vocational/technical, independent study, and special education. There is not a need for more curriculum offerings, but there is a need for refinements.

Some observations and suggestions are as follows: few English teachers enjoy teaching grammar. Those who don't teach grammar probably don't know how to make it meaningful. Spelling must be taught at all grade levels. Social studies teachers must teach citizenship at every grade level. Our form of government is the best when officials use it properly, but a negative attitude by the teacher filters through, perhaps permanently, in turning students against all authority.

Math teachers must teach students the multiplication table, division, fractions, percentages, and other fundamentals necessary for students to become producers and consumers. Public school supervisors and administrators made terrible errors in judgment when they discarded the traditional math programs and installed the "new math." Science teachers must be able to teach a course without the need for an aide. If an aide is required, the course should be modified. I'm sure the English, social studies, math, and foreign language programs would be improved if the board of education gave these departments aides.

Foreign language teachers individually and collectively must publicize the fact that a student must have a knowledge of another language to be a truly educated person. All teachers and supervisors of foreign languages must attempt to introduce these languages in the middle and elementary schools. The other curriculum areas have had to do much of the innovating through the creative teachers working in those subject areas.

The administrator can have a better understanding of the teacher's knowledge of new trends when the teacher informs him through written statements of new techniques and objectives that are being used successfully. It is very helpful if the administrator is made aware of the most recent knowledge in the teacher's field of teaching, and it is also important that the administrator and supervisor understand the teacher's selection of teaching techniques for imparting that knowledge.

THE INSTRUCTIONAL PROGRAM

The teacher has the most important responsibility in the school on a daily basis because he/she must provide the teaching techniques that will motivate each class even though the students in all classes are unique individuals and their attitudes vary period by period.

The teacher must plan each lesson so that specific objectives can be taught during each class period. Some teachers appear to be teaching off the top of their heads when they appear to talk and talk without emphasizing important points. General information has its place, but each class should be aware that they are to master new material daily, and the new material must be taught so that there is continuity and an understanding of the possible applications.

In many classrooms there are students of varied abilities. Gifted, average, slower, retarded, and emotionally disturbed students are present along with potentially disruptive students. The abilities necessary in a teacher to educate this type of class properly requires that he/she have knowledge, patience, and other leadership skills. The same skills are necessary for being a successful administrator, but ironically the skillful teacher usually enjoys remaining in the classroom, and the person who has not been as successful in teaching frequently believes that his/her talents will be useful as an administrator or supervisor.

Boards of education would do well to insist that all people in educational positions continue to use their teaching skills so that the students can profit from other good teaching techniques and also to keep the educators aware of the teaching techniques that are to be used in successful teaching today.

Members of the board of education should be aware of community concerns before adopting programs in sex education and drug abuse. In addition to adopting programs, the board of education must be aware that proper personnel must be available to implement these programs should the board decide the programs are appropriate for their community.

Interscholastic programs featuring athletics, music, dramatics, and club activities are an essential part of the educational program and should be encouraged in order to further develop the skills of those students who have a need for enrichment activities. Activities requiring time are: play rehearsals, band practices, assembly programs, choir rehearsals, pep rallies, class meetings, award programs, public address systems, and team meetings. In fulfilling the time requirements that are suggested to pursue these activities, it must be remembered that the regular academic programs should receive a minimum amount of interruption.

A strong guidance program is necessary at the secondary level. Students must receive direction in applying for college, advanced career training, and in applying for

53

full and part-time jobs. Personal counseling is also very important for students at the secondary level. Since there are many more disruptive students at the secondary and middle school levels, it is wise to hire an additional guidance counselor for the purpose of working daily with the twenty or thirty students who need direction daily. This service should enable the assistant principals to spend more time in classroom settings to help improve instruction.

The library belongs to all school personnel, and it is the responsibility of the management to provide for its maximum usage. Teachers, whenever possible, should be used to help maintain discipline and a quiet library atmosphere.

Team teaching has been used in many ways, some effectively and others horribly. It is not being used effectively when teachers are only teaching two-thirds of the day and are using at least one-sixth of the school day for attending team meetings. It takes very little imagination to realize that planning could take place in the teacher planning period that has been available in nearly every secondary, middle, and junior high school in the country.

For those of you who are unfamiliar with or wonder if there is a difference in the education programs between a middle school and a regular junior high program for grades 6-8, most literature and all personal observations indicate that there is little difference. The regular intermediate program has emphasized rapid growth, learning problems, and curricula which are identical to those of the middle school. Ninth-grade teachers are experiencing many more discipline and student learning problems because most middle schools have reinforced poor habits and attitudes. Middle schools must help teachers control the behavior of students in all classrooms to insure that other students have opportunities to learn.

Class sizes can be large or small for certain types of instruction, but it is not a good policy to place students who learn slowly in a classroom with twenty other students who are difficult to motivate. Gifted, academic, and average students can be taught successfully in a classroom of thirty students, and it is practical to place five slow learning students in an average or academic classroom of twenty-five students and achieve good results. Elementary, middle, and secondary classes have been taught successfully with large enrollments, but a good board of education will insist that the teacher has the opportunity to teach without the interruptions brought about by disruptive students.

Differentiated staffing is a gimmick that can serve no useful purpose and can readily cause divisions in a staff whose teachers should all be capable of leadership roles.

Performance contracting cannot be successful because the personal teacher contact is missing, and the voucher system in addition to causing more desertions from the public schools will cost the taxpayers additional transportation financing.

Teachers are often accused and guilty of using poor teaching techniques. They often:

- refuse to answer students' questions;
- ignore certain students;
- assign too much or no homework;
- use tunnel vision and miss much that takes place in other areas of the room;
- fail to cover important content during the assigned class period, and many students find it difficult to stay after school for make-up work;
- give credit for only a few major tests and give no credit for class participation or

homework;
- fail to collect homework and to correct and return test papers;
- ignore and neglect to report to administrators the student conflicts that they know exist;
- do not teach new material daily;
- are not organized;
- show movie films without previewing the film for the class or without reviewing the film;
- test students on material not assigned or covered in class;
- waste much valuable teaching time in sitting at a desk talking to one student;
- fail to write homework assignments on blackboards or on handout sheets;
- excuse students who return to class after being ill to take a test in another room, and these students are again missing classroom participation;
- lecture and ignore active student participation;
- discipline the whole class instead of the disruptive individuals.

In my estimation the best teacher is not the lecturer or actor. He/she is the person who is able to get participation from all students, even the rebellious ones.

Individualized instruction is another form of overrated education used in the public schools. Individualized instruction is supposedly introduced in the colleges. I have 254 credits, and in every course all college professors used either a lecture or discussion teaching/learning environment. Even in the 1940s professors spoke about individualizing instruction, but no one does, at least at the college level.

In the intermediate and secondary schools some teachers have tried to individualize instruction, and the following weaknesses are frequently ignored or overlooked: the teacher in working with one student is ignoring the other students in the room. The students have no opportunity to learn from interaction with other students in the classroom.

The teacher most frequently serves as a technician rather than a teacher. In other words there is very little teaching. The teacher undoubtedly worked many hours in planning the program, but he/she then believes that the program is all that is needed. The saddest part is that the teacher actually believes that he/she is performing better than the teacher who is getting interaction from students through a variety of carefully chosen teaching approaches and techniques.

When a teacher is able to guide the students as a class, he will have the opportunity to supplement his instruction with a variety of approaches that will provide a much more productive form of individualized instruction. Commercial companies have produced many programs which can be used to supplement learning. In many types of individualized instruction the students are actually covering the same material but in a different sequence or at another time. A better name for this type of instruction is sequenced, not individualized.

Parents are sadly mistaken when they insist on an individualized form of instruction. There are students who are very slow academically, and they are probably learning better in a small class where the teacher is able to offer instruction geared to improving specific reading problems, but the average student learns much more in a class whenever the teacher is capable of inducing interaction among the students in the room.

Science departments have irresponsibly planned outdoor education (camping experiences) for students. Students have missed many valuable learning experiences in English and social studies because the authorities did not consider the consequences of their poor planning. The experience is only worthwhile when all subjects are given equal importance and all teachers, especially those remaining in the school, are not overburdened and can continue to teach.

WHO GOOFED?

Daily we read of turmoil in education. Today there is an emphasis on accountability, but there does not seem to be a reference that boards of education have constructed too many buildings and hired too many people. Many educational programs advocated have been tried and found lacking substance. Schools have been built in wrong areas. The wrong superintendents, administrators, supervisors, teachers, and other employees have been hired.

Now that millions of errors have been committed we can probably regain some of that loss by eliminating some teachers! A teacher formerly taught twenty-five or thirty students and was usually productive; therefore, the teacher today should be equally productive. The students that are in school today in no way, shape, or form resemble yesterday's student. Some students today will go as far as they can to make life miserable for the teacher or anyone else who is in the school.

Parents are reluctant to complain about any problem that occurs in the school, especially those parents who have lived in the school district for a long time. When parents do not speak up about the problems, more serious problems can readily occur.

For example, the following quote appeared in *The Philadelphia Inquirer*:

> A Germantown youth was arrested yesterday and charged with stabbing a Germantown High School teacher Friday during an attempted robbery at the school . . . . *

When teachers cannot walk safely inside any school building, there has to be changes made. The parents can bring about these changes whenever they convince other parents to unite in establishing strong discipline policies.

The answer is that these types of incidents should never occur, but if one does occur then it is the responsibility of the administration to prosecute and to remove the trouble makers from the school district. At no time should a trouble maker be removed from one school in a district and reinstated in another school.

A school district and each separate school within the district must be ever conscious of the problems which exist and must take the necessary steps to correct these problems before the citizens demand and force a change on the administration. Schools should not be coerced into changes when they have had the opportunity to daily observe these disruptions.

Yes, administrators will tell you that there are no disruptions in their schools, but I maintain that disruptions in the educational program occur in most classrooms daily and certainly in all schools.

---

* *The Philadelphia Inquirer*, October 29, 1979, Section B.

In 1976, Frank Manchester, Commissioner for Basic Education, Pennsylvania Department of Education, appointed a statewide task force to study student violence, vandalism, and disruption. It was estimated that nearly $500 million is wasted on vandalism throughout the nation and that there is incalculable education time lost.

$50,000 in subgrants was awarded to eleven school districts and two intermediate units to develop model/demonstration programs. These programs were to develop alternate forms of education to replace suspension and expulsion of students.

Many people believe that students should not be excluded from school since schools are the institutions created to prepare youth for a productive life. The argument sounds logical, but in reality the normal school students are not receiving a decent education because of the disruptions caused by students who are determined that they will do whatever they want to do whenever they want to do it; nevertheless, there can be no denial that society must make a sincere attempt to prepare all youth for a productive life.

Pennsylvania selected small, middle, and large school districts to develop and implement programs of alternate forms of education. The varied approaches include the following actions:

1. An intermediate unit:
   - selected fifty thirteen- and fourteen-year-old disruptive students;
   - used a Self-Control Curriculum designed by Wilkes College personnel to emphasize coping skills and learning strategies in changing behavior of the students.
2. A district:
   - established an on-site center at each of the

four junior high schools;

- provided a different academic program for one-half of each school day. Some students not ready for the regular school day were retained in the on-site center.
- developed a teacher in-service program for discipline.

3. A district:
   - selected sixty of the most disruptive students (truancy and suspension);
   - provided intensive counseling at a community-based site;
   - made personal contacts with parents on a regular basis;
   - provided wilderness trips;
   - selected the ten most disruptive of these sixty students;
   - provided for these ten students one-to-one counseling, group therapy, behavior modification, values clarification, pairings, and simulations.

4. A district:
   - employed three outreach workers to communicate with the students, families, and schools immediately after students had been referred for misbehavior;
   - assigned the outreach workers to use community resources and personnel in helping the referred students to have sense of identity in a large school.

5. A district:
   - established an evaluation team of teachers, counselors, parents, and students;
   - used the team to refer disruptive students to the tutor;

- assigned a counselor to divide her time in working with students in each school;
- required the counselor and tutor to decide when the student is capable of returning to the regularly assigned classes.

6. An intermediate unit servicing twenty-one school districts:
- provided in-service programs for teachers and administrators;
- employed Lehigh University personnel to teach specific diagnostic, remedial, and crisis intervention skills, and the procedures and functions of criminal justice and social agencies within the county;
- trained teachers to assist other teachers;
- used trained teachers to design and staff alternate programs for disruptive students.

7. A district:
- selected eighty disruptive students from grades 9-12 to learn basics of education and vocational development;
- placed those eighty students in a building separate from the regular school setting;
- suggested teachers emphasize values of proper social behavior;
- employed a placement counselor to find employment for these students;
- used a vocational guidance program to teach how to make critical decisions, initiate change, and identify needs.

8. A district:
- provided a self-contained learning center to house thirty-five students;

- selected students by chronological age who were placed academically two years behind other students and placed them in the learning center with other students who were doing poorly;
- added students having social adjustment problems to attend the center;
- assigned personnel to emphasize counseling and student legal responsibilities.

9. A 4,800-student high school:
- provided an in-house suspension room for students who disrupt classes, break windows, assault other students and teachers, cut classes, are truant, etc.;
- evaluated the student's personal and school problems;
- guided the students in coping with the school's requirements and expectations;
- worked with the students' parents;
- assisted in solving home and community problems;
- used community services.

This high school program is to help the 500 students who have been suspended annually (500 disruptive students in one high school).

10. A large district:
- developed a student security aide program to serve in five high schools and one middle school.
- sent a teacher, adult security aide, and students to two camping/workshop settings and also to monthly workshops on law, search and seizure, psychology,

human relationships, and vandalism;

11. A district:
   - selected two teachers and four recent high school graduates to counsel disruptive and alienated students;
   - used the "near peer" counseling program to help students make critical decisions wisely.
   - used "near peer" counseling program to change negative behavior traits of toughness, disruptive behavior, violence, search for danger, etc.

12. A school district:
   - provided teachers and administrators with training not normally provided in teacher preparation programs so that personnel can work more successfully with disruptive students and situations;
   - coordinated the work of and created a common basis of understanding between parents and the school;
   - equipped students with skills necessary to assist each other through personal and situational difficulties.

13. A school district:
   - assigned the social studies department to write units of instruction on vandalism and violence for every grade in the school district.
   - presented an in-service program in September for all teachers in the district.

These thirteen programs selected by the Pennsylvania Department of Education are models to be developed and researched. Other school districts throughout the state are encouraged to study the results and hopefully discover something of value.

In any attempt to adopt an alternative program the best approach is to minimize the number of students to be placed in the group.

Watchung Hills Regional High School, New Jersey, had good success in placing students according to their learning pace. The three rates of learning were (1) fast, (2) normal, (3) and slower. Each English, math, social studies, science, and language teacher assigned a student to a group according to what he/she had learned about the student in his/her classroom. The student could be moved to another group if he/she requested this. Most students at the high school level expect the teacher to place them where they can learn without undue pressure.

North Plainfield School District, New Jersey, adopted a core curriculum that enables the very slow learner to attend English, social studies, and math class during three periods of the day with a teacher capable of helping their academic, social, and other needs. The students are going to other teachers for science, physical education, and electives.

When the needs of the four groups of students listed above (fast, normal, slower, very slow) are met, there will be fewer students referred for classroom disruptions.

Students who have interfered with instruction this school year should be assigned to a teacher capable of establishing a productive relationship. Each grade level should have an English, math, social studies, and science teacher assigned to a classroom for disruptive students. Some disruptive students will be assigned to one of these special teachers for each academic period, while other students may be placed with these special teachers for only one or two periods each day. Students who disrupt classes can be assigned to these special teachers permanently.

School districts bring much unnecessary grief when leaders suggest that students should get a fresh start every fall. Havoc reigns until these students are assigned to teachers who are able to control and teach them. The disruption that these students create will prevent the other students and teachers from progressing normally, if at all. Disruptive students have been placed with teachers randomly or through a computer scheduling. The chronically disruptive student must be with a special teacher beginning with day one of each school year.

When the alternative program of education has been provided, the board of education should not hesitate in adopting practical policies that permit external suspension from school for disruptive students and certainly expulsion procedures for those students who do not change their behavior patterns. Whenever boards of education have the courage to provide guidelines to remove these rebellious students, they find that the students will gain outstanding learning environments, the teachers will enjoy teaching without disturbances, the administrators will not be tied down and can help to improve instruction, and the laymen can be pleased in knowing that the public schools are finally functioning properly.

PERSONNEL

Public school employees must understand the importance of the people in a school district. It has been a belief of a superintendent and expressed to me that students and parents are only here for two or three years and they move, but the teacher will always be here and he/she is the one who must be satisfied! This is a classic example of establishment self-perpetuity.

We must remember that the priority in education is to satisfy the students who are here for the purpose of receiving a good education. The teachers are the second most important people because they are directly working with all of the students and their influence is most important. The other personnel are supportive, and each one must play some part in helping the teacher to have a conducive learning environment.

The teacher should be able to use at least 99 percent of each period for teaching. Most administrators believe that the teacher should handle all discipline problems, and they refuse to discipline the students who are creating

68

problems. A wise board of education member will insist that all administrators support the policies that have been adopted.

It is agreed that some teachers are apt to send too many students to the office, but it is the administrator's job to get to the classroom to assist the teacher in improving his/her techniques so that referrals will be minimal. The administrator is also to be aware that some students will not easily change their behavior and that the administrator will need to remove the students from the classroom and school if there is no rapid behavior change.

Effective educational leadership will be promoted by increasing the teacher's knowledge of individual differences of his/her students. Many teachers do not possess this knowledge, even though pupils are the most important part of the education. The teacher-pupil contact that occurs daily is the most important aspect of the educational environment. The dinner table in many homes is the setting for, "What happened in school today, John?"

John could mention that his teacher was unfair to him in grading a paper, that he had no opportunity to ask questions, that the teacher can't control the class, or a thousand other things that teachers are careless about.

John might reiterate some of the succulent gossip that his teacher expressed about other students, teachers, administrators, or school board members.

He might mention that he couldn't see his teacher after school for extra help because his teacher was to attend a teachers' meeting on salary negotiations.

The teacher who is so negligent and so critical of other professionals is in many cases the same individual who is taking bows as a member of the teachers' advisory team because he believes that his salesmanship is helping the teachers. The teacher who is dedicated to helping students and is aware of teaching profession ethics is the person who advances the status of the public schools.

The teacher who is respected by the students for his/her fairness, sincerity, and affection is the teacher who does most for the profession because his/her dedication is expressed to listening parents at the dinner table. The friendly school personnel who reach people through church, service clubs, neighborhood gatherings, and school extracurricular activities are the people who help the school improve its rating in the community.

The administrator who clearly understands his responsibilities will assist teachers with their concerns regarding the teaching and discipline problems occurring in the classrooms, cafeteria, and halls, and he will do so everyday.

Teachers must receive direction in handling student-parent-teacher conferences because much derogatory publicity results whenever the school personnel will not listen or make any attempt to reach a compromise. Administrators often assume the same uncompromising posture, and I believe that much of this exists because the board of education supports the permissive attitude of leaving it to the professional. "We will support all of your decisions. What do we know?!"

School boards should not permit administrators to duplicate assignments. For example, a school district will employ a supervisor for English, social studies, science, math, etc., and they also employ a curriculum coordinator to coordinate what's left, but there's nothing left! The principal of each school provides the master schedule which records the classes scheduled for each subject area. The classes scheduled for each subject area have been approved by the supervisor. Why have a curriculum coordinator? If you have a curriculum coordinator, then please get rid of the supervisors.

Even though orientation of a teacher to a new position is extremely important, management makes little or no effort to see that this is accomplished properly. Mistakes are made through no fault of the teacher.

Some teachers who prove most capable are taken advantage of and given the more difficult teaching and related assignments year after year. This is certainly an area that can be used by the board of education to award those capable teachers for the job that they do. This is a form of merit that can be easily defended.

It is the direct responsibility of the person assigned to handle personnel to insure that he understands a ten-year long-range program so that teachers are not hired one year and dismissed a short time later through no fault of the teacher.

Personnel in education as well as in business are not conscious of the ethics that should be part of their professional career. Stories told in confidence are magnified and retold to department chairpersons or administrators, who become bitter toward some teacher because some prejudiced faculty member has spoken unfairly. Beginning and new teachers must be very careful what they say to other teachers. Stories become twisted and magnified.

Administrators must organize and follow a work schedule. Questions directed at the administrator can elicit responses which may convince you that he has developed a stable form of organization, that the school building has everything, and that he has a good staff. But is he organized?

Even though it is extremely important to design a workable plan or organization and to provide the building and facilities that will meet the needs of the community, it is even more important to develop employees who can work with children and other school personnel. Personnel should be developed, not fired. Uncooperative personnel should be fired.

School board members must select employees objectively. Although it is easy and proper to fire personnel who do not perform well, responsible administrators and supervisors must first make efforts to improve the teaching performances.

All teaching positions are important; therefore, in selecting teachers the board of education must be careful to choose those people who are flexible enough in their thinking to indicate that necessary adjustments can be made immediately. Individual characteristics, background, and experience must be weighed carefully.

It is possible to develop personnel into meeting job requirements if the principal is conscious of the assignments to be performed. Although schools have set up programs that are meant to develop personnel, I believe that a principal, with a reasonable amount of time and effort, can better initiate a program for improvement.

School costs are most expensive for buildings, transportation, and personnel. Many school boards have been negligent in overspending for buildings and transportation.

Selecting personnel becomes an even greater responsibility when you consider that the normal promotion will be awarded to a member of the existing staff. The school board must offer present members of the staff a sincere interview, but qualified candidates should receive equal opportunity.

Some schools are fortunate in having a director of personnel who can visit college campuses and other schools to interview and observe candidates. Regardless of the capabilities of the director, it is normal routine for other personnel to serve major responsibilities in interviewing and hiring practices.

Some schools located in more favorable environments frequently do not recruit because the number of candidates in those areas is more than enough to fill all local jobs. This in-breeding should be discouraged because an evaluation of these types of systems evince less progressive teaching methods, complacency, and political promotions in most cases of advancement.

In recruiting it is very important that the future goals of the candidates be ascertained. It is very likely that recruitment of great numbers of teachers desiring to leave the teaching field for administrative or supervisory positions could leave a school system with too many inexperienced teachers.

The thorough recruiting job that can be accomplished by a principal or director is too important to refer to a superintendent of schools who has too many other assignments and too little time to observe teachers to do a competent recruiting job. The superintendent is also too far removed from the teaching-learning situation to do an excellent job, but I realize that many superintendents are reluctant to yield this responsibility, and the students might again be denied the opportunity to learn from different teaching techniques.

It is extremely undesirable for school systems to advertise for candidates when the officials already have made a decision on the replacement. This occurs because board of education members appear to be impressed when the administration lists a large number of applicants for a position. Administrations advertise for coaches, and, even though other applicants have better backgrounds, they contend their assistant is best! In hiring leadership personnel from outside, it is essential that the selected person be chosen more for his decision making and administering change than for his college transcript or number of degrees.

Recruiters are most unethical in exchanging information concerning candidates. Recruiters have come to a
school district after they have already decided to hire a
teacher or administrator! They visit, I have discovered,
not to get reliable recommendations, but to gain more
favor with the school board members back in their own
district. Needless to say, a school official will not give any
reliable information to the recruiter because he/she
realizes that the recruiter does not want to hear anything
negative, and the school official could be burned by the
unethical practices of the recruiter if he/she does mention
any negative characteristic of the person who, for all
practical purposes, has been hired.

A teacher, coach, and administrator quickly learn that
recommendations given in all truthfulness and with an attempt to help the prospective employer make a more objective decision are not held in confidence by the
employer! Many employers will not thank you, nor do
they want you to mention anything other than words of
congratulations for the selection that they have undoubtedly made.

I hope that employers in business and government are
much more professional in receiving recommendations
than the unethical personnel who are so numerous in
education and athletics.

Far too frequently the new teacher or guidance
counselor discovers that he/she is criticized for not doing
assignments that were evidently not pointed out to
him/her. A job analysis should be available for all school
personnel so that the employee can prepare for handling
the tasks that were not covered in the college classroom
or during student teaching. Even the experienced teacher
when placed in an unfamiliar position will need a job
analysis and supervision.

Teachers in the school have the most unethical professional habit of reporting to the administration that another teacher left the classroom with paper lying around the room, that the blackboards had not been erased, etc. The professional approach of direct contact with the other teacher probably could have solved the problem, but in many instances the administration is at fault for not having developed a program to inform the teachers that they have many obligations to perform other than in the instructional area.

Far too many teachers in the public schools have the attitude that they have been hired as classroom teachers only. Hallways, study hall, cafeteria, assemblies, and other types of student activities are all part of the public school educational program, and teacher supervision is expected. Many teachers accept these responsibilities graciously, and some take extra steps because they are really professional and do not need to be asked.

Most teachers have been very diligent in transmitting content knowledge to their students but in doing so have often neglected to impart to the students that the attitudes of willing cooperation, proper respect for authority, respect for other people's traditions, respect for parents, church, and government, and concern for their own spiritual life are moral values that should be developed.

The administration should hold faculty meetings on a regular basis, at which time an agenda, with prior contributions made by the teachers, can give direction in enabling all members of the staff to understand their responsibilities and to have some share in reaching an agreement of the objectives to be achieved. In addition to promulgating the specific objectives of the school district, the administration must use small and individual conferences to discuss additional knowledge, teaching skills, human relation attitudes, appropriate discipline procedures, and community relationships.

Local professionals should be used: police, firemen, college professors, state representatives, local politicians, physicians, and other specialists can offer expertise and positive communication relationships.

A practice frequently used in order to free a new teacher from the sometimes overbearing pressures is for an administrator to offer a reduced teaching load and/or supplementary assignment load until the new teacher has had more time to adjust to his new duties. Tact must be used in introducing this approach because there are many teachers and organizations that will insist on equality of work loads.

The board of education must insist that the observation and evaluation system be used daily if the school district is to fulfill its stated objective of improving classroom instruction. The teacher who is visited frequently will continue to improve as a teacher. Observers must help him/her to develop his/her teaching techniques and to support him/her in improving student behavior. A teacher who is probably worth $8,000 as a teacher to a school district can become as good a teacher in a very short period of time as a $16,000 teacher when he/she receives the supervision that a school district must provide. Classroom supervision is the secret; not office, golf course, or telephone supervision.

Another way in which boards of education can save money is personally to check the teaching schedules of all employees. I am familiar with a school hiding four extra teachers by assigning a number of teachers as resource teachers or placing them in the same classroom to teach when another teacher was actually already teaching in that classroom. Very deceitful, don't you agree?

Usually a board of education will mandate that fifteen or more students be assigned to a classroom; however, I have made classroom observations in which six or eight students were assigned. Quite often, I might add.

In any development program the supervisor or administrator should encourage the teacher to take opportunities to be innovative, scientific, and creative if he/she is to improve as a teacher. The secret, of course, is that the supervisor or administrator can be a better leader if he/she is also intelligent, cooperative, and creative.

The resource people in the local community must be reached for the knowledge and skills that they can offer to the students. Some resource people have encouraged and led students into a new vocation and frequently have changed attitudes.

J. Galen Saylor has stated: "The possibility of using community people as resource persons is limited only by the special competencies of the local citizens, and the ingenuity of school personnel in using them."[*]

The teachers, supervisors, and administrators are able to contact and use the proper community resource people, but the program should be coordinated in order that the same resource is not taken advantage of and other resource people have an equal opportunity to contribute their talents.

Students have been able to learn self-defense, first aid, life-saving techniques, guitar, piano, and many other skills related to career and avocational pursuits from citizens in the surrounding communities.

In many public schools there are teachers who have talents that should be used for teaching students after school, in the late afternoon or early evening. There is little reason why the student cannot pay for this education, especially since the teacher is giving up recreational or rest time. The school district has the responsibility of evaluating the suggested activity because there could be

---

[*]J. Galen Saylor and William M. Alexander, *Curriculum Planning for Modern Schools* (New York: Holt, Rinehart and Winston, 1966), p. 474.

outside commercial concerns.

The teacher should be receiving literature and in-service information concerning:

- new trends in teaching methods and curriculum;
- school budgets and building programs;
- staff regulations and policies;
- social events;
- academic and athletic news;
- school district calendar;
- guidance information;
- community information;
- communication aids;
- strengths and needs of the school;
- discipline and school law.

The teacher has 180 teaching days during the school year, and it is unlikely that an evaluator will see or understand all of the various types of written, oral, and visual means of communication that the teacher will use during the other 898 unobserved periods. The effectiveness of the ways in which those communication skills are used cannot be ascertained by an evaluator who only observes the teaching during part of one or two teaching periods.

How do you evaluate a teacher who is not very successful in supervising a large group of students who are usually assigned to a cafeteria or study hall but is capable of teaching successfully in a regular classroom? This teacher may not be able to handle a large group of students, and the administration must be careful to protect itself by assigning a teacher who is capable of controlling those students. I believe that you will find by examining most evaluation systems that there are teachers who are rated outstanding even though they are not able to control students unless they have the power to pass or fail them in a regular classroom. Are these teachers really as good as the teachers who can handle any situation?

In addition to evaluating the teaching staff the board of education should offer a reasonable explanation for employing elementary, middle, intermediate, junior high, and even some high school administrators during summer months. Central office staff certainly have much less work to do during summer months.

If a board of education does not have an administrator capable of doing all the work in two weeks of summer employment, they better get someone who can. A high school should have a principal and an assistant available throughout the summer (of course, they get vacations, too) but there is no reason why the citizens permit the board of education to throw literally thousands of dollars away when there is no reason for it. This loss of money has been going on for many years.

Seniority has taken preference over other qualities in most promotions. Experience dictates that, since the student is the most important person in the school system, the official selecting supervisory, administrative, and other leaders in education should choose the person who is most capable of working with these students. Objective evaluations supersede seniority.

Democratic leadership should be used in advancing all personnel; however, it should be considered that proper criteria will help to reduce the subjectivity accompanying any promotion. Far too frequently one person on the staff decides that his/her best friend is the best and only qualified person. Any promotion in the school district should be based on the evaluation ratings and on the interviews conducted by a committee of the board of education. At the interviews the committee must objectively determine what the candidate has done for the students and what he/she intends to accomplish in the vacant position.

Boards of education should establish criteria to inform all teaching personnel of the requirements necessary to receive certification in supervisory and administrative positions. Competition will eliminate some self-perpetuity.

It is evident from a study of the history of public education that there is a stereotyping perpetuated because the personnel in management positions have asked the teaching personnel who think in similar fashion to take courses in supervision and administration.

A neophyte in management circles very quickly learns that there are definite methods to be used and that there is very little opportunity to use methods that would in any way tend to "rock the boat."

A superintendent, acting superintendent, and principal have made it very clear to me that they wanted everything learned and performed exactly as it has always been; in fact, one of them said that no one should be hired for an administrative position from outside the district since he would not be familiar with school district policy! Congratulations to the board of education that had the wisdom to hire a person with that type of decision-making ability!

In business certain methods are used to bring about a rapid or gradual rise in productivity, and the business must use new ideas if it is to be competitive, but in the field of education there are no competitive factors to be concerned with. Anyone who attempts to correct the faults of public school education quickly learns that he/she is not in step and is in a losing situation.

If someone in a management team believes that another school has a new and possibly workable program, it may be possible to sell that program so that it can be implemented, but you must remember that the program to be adopted must fall within the philosophy of public school education that appears to be more concerned with preserving management's interests than in rectifying the faults of the well-established system. Few leaders permit innovating by subordinates.

The boards of education literally throw away taxpayers' money in sending administrators and supervisors who live on the East Coast to California and Texas for conferences and sending administrators and supervisors who live on the West Coast to New York and Florida! Since education is a state function and not a federal function, common sense would dictate having necessary conferences (most are not worth the time and energy) within the state's boundaries at some convenient location.

The department of education in each state should have the responsibility for knowing what is taking place around the country and for transmitting this information to the school districts via mailed literature or convenient conferences.

Administrators and supervisors have been attending conferences for years, every year. Has the board of education any evidence of how the information garnered has been used? Have other school personnel been able to review the notes obtained at these conferences? What benefits have the students gained from these conferences?

Much has been written about personnel appraisal techniques. These include:

- teacher self-evaluation;
- ratings of teachers by pupils;
- ratings of teachers by school administrators;
- evaluation by supervisors;
- evaluation of teachers by colleagues;

- evaluation of teachers by outside professional experts;
- evaluation of teachers by special committees;
- evaluation of teachers by lay citizens;
- evaluation of teachers through their classroom instruction;
- evaluation of teachers through cumulative personnel records;
- teacher evaluation based on pupil changes;
- evaluation of teachers on the basis of nonstructured written responses; and
- evaluation of teachers by means of questionnaires and examinations.[*]

Although all of the above appraisals have merit, my opinion is that a more thorough supervision program should be implemented that will give a more realistic appraisal of personnel and thereby enable a school to adopt a positive retention program.

A supervisory program that separates the supervision from administrative responsibilities is not fair to the community. If supervision is unable to bring forth outstanding teaching, it is the responsibility of the administrator to recommend accordingly; therefore, it is indefensible to separate a principal from an important function in his normal assignment. All administrators must supervise classroom teaching.

---

[*]Jefferson N. Eastmond, *The Teacher and School Administration* (Boston: Houghton Mifflin, 1959), pp. 402-407. See also Robert B. Howsam, *Who's A Good Teacher? Problems and Progress in Teacher Evaluation* (Burlingame, Calif.: California Teachers Association, 1960). See also William B. Castetter, *Administering the School Personnel Program* (Toronto: Macmillan, 1962), pp. 286-287.

Supervisory functions daily performed are the best guide to an effective retention program. In performing supervisory functions a good administrator will:

- demonstrate the proper techniques in a classroom setting;
- observe the teacher and suggest alternatives to be selected by the teacher for achieving better results;
- follow the teacher for a day as he/she goes through his/her assignments;
- maintain records of all observations and suggestions;
- develop personnel for advancement and for full effectiveness in their present position;
- communicate continually with all staff members to maintain loyalty and support of administrative policies;
- obtain resources to provide training;
- conduct in-service training and provide additional time for staff members to relate to each other;
- hold group conferences so that objectives and methods can be reinforced or changed;
- employ informal meetings to encourage staff members to relate their problems more immediately, receive an answer, and return to their work enthusiastically;
- create a development program for assisting administrators, supervisors, and teachers to learn more about the skills necessary to be successful in their field;
- provide job descriptions for all school personnel.

- enable a teacher to observe a department head or another teacher as a learning model. Be sure to provide all teachers with this type of opportunity;
- encourage joint discussion among administrators, supervisors, and teachers in agreeing on objectives;
- rotate the department chairman assignment to improve the morale of all teachers and to allow each teacher the opportunity to lead;
- provide more leadership positions at various levels because people who have responsibility work more effectively. This can be accomplished without an appreciable increase in cost;
- study the qualifications for advancement which must take into consideration job experience, college courses, leadership potential, and public relations already exhibited;
- give a periodic statement of individual performance to all personnel observed. List suggestions for improvement;
- rate an observed person according to the objectives that have been stated in the teacher's plan book. A teacher should not receive recognition for a "canned lesson";
- rate supervisors and administrators according to their job description requirements and work schedule to be followed;
- plan a development program that will provide your school district with adequate replacements should administrative or supervisory employees move out of the school district; and
- use objective plans and methods in evaluat-

ing all school personnel. The teacher's preparation, teaching techniques, and student reaction must be recorded for the period of the observation. In arriving at an overall evaluation, all areas of the teacher's contributions must be assessed. An overall evaluation of the teacher should never be compared with other teachers' ratings unless teachers are to be eliminated from the staff.

Since results are paramount, it is essential that the administrator evaluate his/her performance in the previously stated parts of the program. If any part of the evaluation has not been performed objectively or democratically, the retention process will be structurally weakened.

A principal working full time is necessary to insure fair evaluation. The administrator's philosophy is an important consideration. Education has been seriously impeded by administrators who have not kept abreast of the responsibilities that accompany leadership. Instead of being prodded by irate parents, rebellious students, and disgruntled taxpayers, the principal should be exploring new horizons, having already surmounted the tasks that are even now facing the typical administrator.

A board of education, in order to prescribe policy, must have all essential information at its fingertips. The superintendent should insist on all personnel having major responsibility report the progress at a conference session. A board member who hears a report directly will become more involved; therefore, he/she will be a better board member.

Public schools need democratic leadership which will encourage all teachers to be more creative. Believing that teachers appreciate help when it is offered tactfully, the principal would be able to improve the teaching/learning situation and to raise the morale. The teachers should be more interested in providing success experiences for all students than in setting high standards which prove impossible for some youth to reach. Low morale results when the teacher is not firm and fair, but there are many teachers who prefer to be "one of the boys" and are usually inconsistent in disciplining misbehaving students.

Changes in the curriculum can be best advanced by the teacher who will experiment in his classroom. Additions to the curriculum should eventually supplement the present curriculum, but an enormous amount of change will occur when the teacher realizes that the student must become more involved in dialogue and activity.

A teacher has a very important decision to make in many school districts today. Having to work with colleagues, he/she believes that he/she must function as a team member. What if the association or union decides to strike?

I faced that situation in a school district; two of us believed that it was not professional to interfere with the academic and extracurricular activities of the students so there was no strike. At that time I also felt that I had a responsibility to support the board and administration because I believed they were honest and would only do what was best. After having the opportunity to work with management, I realize how wrong I was; however, I remain firm in believing that at no time should the students be used as a pawn in a conflict between the teachers and the board of education. I am not implying that all boards of education and administrators are dishonest, but I can recall working for people who displayed much stupidity, arrogance, and dishonesty. Although I have never missed a day of work since I began in January 1948, there were many days and evenings when I felt extremely uncomfortable in being associated with these unethical misfits in public school education. I'm talking about board members and administrators.

Boards of education have made many costly mistakes, and the job of the board today is to correct those mistakes without running roughshod over the teachers, who usually are the scapegoat for somebody else's mistakes.

Personnel, of course, is always the heart of any organization, and, in education where so many lives are being molded daily, it is most essential that recruitment and hiring be a high priority for the board of education. If the members use their intelligence and hire wisely, there is less chance that they will be so quick to drop teachers for no particular reason other than there are a few less students today.

The proper development of teachers rests with the supervisors and administrators. My experience is that teachers really are interested in doing a good job and that they will work to correct problems if the problems are pointed out professionally. It is frequently said that there are many poor teachers. If there are, then it is the responsibility of management to help these teachers to be good. An administrator who does not do his job in helping to improve instruction is a poor administrator, and a board of education that allows such negligence to happen is an incompetent board of education.

The most ridiculous situation occurring in education, and one that is so asinine that I have to laugh even though it is not humorous, is a principal who rants and raves every time that he is challenged. Because he throws a temper tantrum, the board members are frightened, and the teachers, realizing the power that this administrator is able to abuse, are also fearful.

Teachers are not always aware of the relationships that exist in their classrooms. Teachers are usually thinking of the content, techniques, and other interests, and they do not always realize the respect that students hold for them.

In McCaskey High School, Lancaster, Pennsylvania, I had a homeroom teacher who, I thought, was most appealing. One day someone in the room threw chalk against the blackboard when the teacher was out of the room. When she returned and saw chalk on the floor she, being upset, asked what had happened. I did not know or I would have told her because I did respect authority and would have considered that type of behavior most childish. A girl told the teacher that I had thrown the chalk. I believe that the girl actually thought that I had done it because when she turned around once during the period, I had been staring in her direction. Actually, I had looked in her direction because at the time she looked attractive. Circumstantial evidence made me look guilty in the eyes of the girl, and the teacher certainly had no reason to doubt the girl's truthfulness.

You can imagine how painful it must have been for a young man in his senior year of high school to be depicted as a jerk, sneak, and liar! After all these years I remember that incident, and even after all the years have passed I hope that someday I can tell my *favorite* teacher that things are not always as they appear to be and that I regret that I did not go out of my way to tell her how hurt I was by being rejected at that time.

NEGOTIATIONS

Public school teachers have in many school districts been most successful in receiving a salary comparable to employees in business with similar degrees of education. There have been very few attempts to determine objectively the salaries that should be paid to personnel in public schools. As a citizen, you have the responsibility to know exactly what benefits the board of education has awarded to the teachers, management, secretaries, and custodial staff.

In most negotiating for secretarial and custodial staffs there is very little analysis of the tasks performed and the manner in which they have been performed. There should be evaluations of all staff members so that they can be paid according to the work produced. The type of work performed by these people is very similar to the work that is a part of the business world and can be scaled similar to work in civil service areas.

An assistant superintendent or someone in the central office possessing a similar educational background should represent the board of education in negotiations with the teaching staff. A person familiar with all areas of the local school district should certainly be more fruitful for the school district to employ as a negotiator. Colleges offer courses which school districts should use in developing negotiators. Any analysis of present contracts certainly does not indicate wise bargaining.

The contributions made by administrators, supervisors, and teachers must be assessed according to the needs of the educational program. The board of education must adopt a salary guide that provides financial incentives for those teachers who are capable and do take the most difficult assignments.

If positions are to be dropped, personnel who have served the district well should be given every opportunity to serve the district in a financially comparable position, preferably as a teacher. Teachers with less seniority are released. With students needing more attention and more alternative programs, the talents of these successful people should be used in building the instructional program. Attrition is the only fair system to use in correcting the problems that a previous board of education has permitted to occur.

Public school teachers and their negotiators have fought to receive a free period each day. Some attempt is made to fit it into the teaching schedule by calling this period a planning period. Even though there is some use of the period to discuss curriculum with other teachers, the teachers who are professional will admit that most teachers merely use the time for socializing or relaxing.

In most schools the teacher will teach five 45-minute classes, supervise one class period, have one free period, and eat for thirty minutes. The 6.75 hours required to be in school with only 5.5 hours left for teaching and supplementary assignments does not give the teacher much of a teaching day, does it? Negotiations should provide all teachers with the most pleasant working conditions and conducive teaching environments, but I see no reason why the teachers should not have the stamina or interest to work a full day of 6.25 hours. Administrators desiring popularity have traditionally been granting this free time, and the boards of education rubber stamp. Competency?

That teachers often will not meet with parents beyond the regular school hours is another measure of the way in which boards of education have permitted unstructured recruitment of teachers.

Isn't the situation ridiculous when teachers are more concerned with fighting to do less work instead of trying to find more ways that they can help the students? Teachers should make an attempt to receive a better salary and fringe benefits, but to be in a profession and expect to work less than 6.25 hours is a definite indication of laziness.

ATHLETIC PROGRAM

A comprehensive athletic program affords many opportunities for students to acquire skills that will serve them in adulthood. Athletic activities that do not have carry-over value should be considered for the physical, mental, emotional, and social attributes that are necessary in helping to serve more fully the needs of the competitive youth. Some of these sports have the advantage of being performed before thousands of spectators.

An athletic program must have leadership and direction to be effective. The administration's policies must be broad enough for an athletic director to work under, but the principal must be alert enough to enter the picture should the program fail to develop.

Since the principal has the responsibility for the activities of the school, he/she must be careful in selecting someone who will make decisions. All head coaches are responsible for decisions, and an athletic director should likewise be responsible for supervising the athletic program. The athletic director should be paid for supervising athletic contests and observing coaches performing their assignments. He/she should not be given released class-time but should be a regular teaching member of the school faculty. It is much more reasonable for a board of education to pay an athletic director by the hour. Scheduling of buses and ordering of equipment should also be performed by the athletic director. If the athletic director would perform these duties adequately, the principal should provide him with a business manager to aid in handling the selling of tickets.

Boards of education should be working to include all sports for which there is a genuine interest among the student body. Established sports must not be hindered by added others that will negate or hinder the plus factors already existing in the successful activities. Space, facilities, finances, and teaching personnel available must be considered factors before enlarging the athletic program. Title IX requirements also must be followed.

Even though the coaches of the girls' and boys' teams must be given the opportunity to express their needs and suggestions, it is most important that the boards of education provide administrators or athletic directors to make decisions that will provide equal opportunities for all participants.

Far too frequently the board of education does not provide sufficient custodial staff to maintain and upgrade the outdoor playing areas, and the teams must participate on extremely rough and dangerous terrain and on improperly marked surfaces.

Efforts must be made to provide equitable remuneration for personnel who are coaching athletic activities that require more technical skills and insight. Whenever performances are to be advanced and safety risks accompany that improvement, then the outstanding coaches must be acknowledged. Wrestling and gymnastics are athletic activities that require the teaching of more technical skills, and yet the coaches are not normally paid as well because the sports are not the prestige activities.

The public schools are learning that many teachers are not interested in serving as athletic coaches. Many of the qualified coaches have decided to abandon coaching duties, and the other teachers are unable or unwilling to coach. Girls and boys will lose many opportunities to participate because athletic activities will be curtailed or eliminated whenever personnel are unavailable.

Boards of education will be pressured into providing each coach with a "feeding system." The pros and cons are debatable, especially since some systems have proved to be unsuccessful. Boards of education should be concerned with the type of extracurricular activities in the elementary schools, but they should be more concerned with the type of activities and level of skills being taught in the physical education classes of those schools. Students should be taught early to enjoy physical exercise. Most citizens have weight problems because physical educators and health teachers did not emphasize the value of continuing to exercise.

Although a varied skills program should be taught, instructors should be encouraged to stress skills that will teach speed, strength, and agility. Educators have been known to exclude basketball games from the class skills because students have an opportunity to play this game outside of school. Possibly some students do, but I believe that all students should have this opportunity under a capable instructor. Wrestling has been excluded because of injuries when better supervision would rectify the situation. It is, of course, the duty of the administration to have instructors capable of teaching the fundamentals of all varsity activities. If only football fundamentals are taught, the high school soccer coach will complain.

All coaches and department heads should be evaluated constantly because it is the administration's job to provide the best situation possible for each sport, even though such a responsibility may require the athletic director and the principal to ruffle the ego of the less skillful coach. Many coaches have had little experience in college athletic programs and will need much supervision.

The health and safety of students is another area in which the board of education must assume a leadership role.

Each year throughout the country athletes are receiving serious and unnecessary injuries because of equipment and dirty coaching techniques. In the 1950s football squads began to have all players wear face guards. Prior to this only a player with a broken nose or a player who needed eye-glass coverage wore a face mask.

Today all players are being equipped with face guards which give them the false impression that they will not be injured. Without a face guard a defender must use more skill and courage in tackling, but in doing so he does not expose himself to a crippling injury, nor does he strike his opponent with such violence that someone can be maimed or killed. To understand this more fully, place your face in front of a person running toward you. It is natural to turn your face aside. Now, place a face guard in front of your nose; you will not turn your head to the side, and you will hit the person head on with a violent force.

Coaches recognize the dangers inherent with face masks, and many have suggested that face masks be removed from the helmets. Teachers and coaches are very much limited in their authority but the boards of education could demand a study (many have been made by physicians and trainers) and take the necessary action of having face guards removed.

Some coaches have instructed their players in using the forearm lift to bring it up hard against the nose, jaw, or face of the opponent. There is no place for violent coaches in the profession, but, since they are already there, I would recommend that the forearm lift be abolished by changing the football rule book. Face masks came into use because coaches had instructed (demanded) that their players strike a forearm blow to the face. Yes, many coaches teach violence!

CONSTITUTION AND INTERPRETATION

All policies, rules, and regulations adopted by school personnel must be in compliance with federal and state constitutional law. The constitutional rights as enumerated in the First and Fourteenth Amendments to the United States Constitution are important to understand because these are the laws which govern many students' and teachers' concerns today.

The Constitution states in Amendment I that: "Congress shall make no law respecting an establishment of religion or prohibiting the free exercise thereof; or abridging the freedom of speech or of the press; or of the right of the people to assemble, and to petition the government for a redress of grievances."

Amendment XIV states:

> All persons born or naturalized in the United States, and subject to the jurisdiction thereof, are citizens of the United States and of the State wherein they reside. No State shall make or en-

force any law which shall abridge the privileges or immunities of citizens of the United States; nor shall any State deprive any person of life, liberty or property without due process of law; nor deny to any person within its jurisdiction the equal protection of the laws.

The right of public school students to freedom of speech was affirmed by the United States Supreme Court in the case of *Tinker* v. *Des Moines Community School District*, 393 U.S. 503 (1969), where the Court said:

It can hardly be argued that students or teachers shed their constitutional rights to freedom of expression at the school house gate. Students in school as well as out of school are persons under the Constitution. They are possessed of fundamental rights which the State must respect, just as they themselves must respect their obligations to the State. In our system, students may not be regarded as closed-circuit recipients of only that which the State chooses to communicate. They may not be confined to the expression of those sentiments that are officially approved. In the absence of a specific showing of constitutionally valid reasons to regulate their speech students are entitled to freedom of expression of their views.

This right is qualified, however. The U.S. Supreme Court stated:

But conduct by the student, in class or out of it, which for any reason — whether it stems from time, place, or type of behavior — materially disrupts classwork or involves substantial disorder or invasion of the rights of others, is, of course, not immunized by the constitutional guarantee of freedom of speech.

Students misinterpret the freedom of speech guarantee and not so politely inform the teacher that they can say anything they desire because they have freedom of speech. This abuse of a freedom definitely interferes with the teaching environment, places unneeded additional stress on the teacher, and infringes on the amount of learning offered to all students.

Due process of law is a right entitled to all employees under Amendment XIV. Superintendents and boards of education have proved to be incompetent in demoting employees or taking away their jobs without providing the legal rights that the Constitution of the United States mandates. It is almost unbelievable that something as serious as this can occur in public school education. Guilty parties should atone for their federal crime.

The Fifth Amendment to the Constitution of the United States is used and misused daily in the schools. The amendment which protects the citizen from incriminating himself is frequently ignored in the schools. The teacher or administrator will ask the student, "Did you smoke that cigarette?" If the student says, "Yes," he will be suspended. If the student lies, he will not be punished; therefore, the student is encouraged to lie. No one should ever subject a student to committing a sin to avoid discipline or a family confrontation. Schools must not limit Fifth Amendment rights only to criminal cases.

Laws to protect citizens' rights are necessary, but federal intervention in the administering of public education will probably erode even more since the president of the United States has advocated a powerful and separate department for education. It would be interesting to know who the advisers are who are able to persuade our leaders to build additional bureaucracies when experience has indicated that any department to justify its existence will expand duties, and this department will be allowed to dictate unreasonable changes to a school board that has not done its homework or one that is typically afraid to defend the rights of the people that have been challenged by an intolerant federal agency. Will Reagan abolish or modify this power?

HEW, a federal agency designed to protect the interests of citizens who are being discriminated against, came to our school district because someone had told them that some students were not receiving an equal education.

Ten members of a committee representing HEW visited our school district for two days to observe our two high schools. They actually took the time (about one half hour) to sit down with our administrators, and during this time they told us that the alternative form of education which provided two teachers for seven students was not viable! The federal agency was not interested in accepting the fact that these students refused to go into classrooms in the regular high schools. The committee was not willing to hear that the students were receiving individual instruction and guidance. The only alternative left for a school district was to expel those students. The committee offered no solution.

The committee stressed that they were interested in seeing our student records for discipline. As you can well imagine, the committee never came near my office, nor did it look at discipline records in any other office in our school. The message is that school boards must put pressure on legislators and the executive branch to curb bigoted committees that are using tax money to accomplish little that is helpful to anyone in public education.

At a Pennsylvania Department of Education conference designed to provide information for administrators who were interested in alternative forms of education, a highly prejudiced state department official spoke critically of a western Pennsylvania school district because he had heard that school authorities in that public school district were hurting minority students. This occurred just after the public school district had presented, in detail, what they were doing to help unsuccessful school students get a better education. Evidently, the official believed the wrong students would be placed in the alternate educational program.

After learning that the state official had not visited that school district, I arose to chastise him for not investigating that school district before he rendered his judgment and also for being critical of those school personnel who were selected to present their school district program at a state conference. These people implement programs; they are not necessarily responsible for the design and adoption.

MORAL, LEGAL, AND HEALTH CONCERNS

The board of education is responsible for establishing policies in all areas of education. An area that receives very little emphasis is the moral behavior of school personnel. The public schools, especially since most states have lawyers demanding this, have published discipline codes applicable for students.

Admittedly the administrators, supervisors, teachers, and custodians are old enough to purchase alcoholic beverages. I hope they are never feeble enough to require the use of drug controlled substances, but some school personnel do use them. Students are suspended, removed from extra-curricular activities, expelled from school, and at times incarcerated. School personnel appear to be exempt!

There are principals, assistant principals, teachers and custodians who at times, in my presence, were in an area or had a body odor that reeked of alcohol or smoke. These school personnel are not only around their peers, but they are also around students. I have been with administrators who were so much under the influence of alcohol at dances and other extracurricular activities that the conditions demand correction.

Everyone understands that the assistant principals are responsible for enforcing abuses among the student body. Who is responsible for enforcing abuses or, quite rightfully, any use of alcohol when an administrator or teacher steps on school property?

The board of education must establish policies that can be implemented. The policies cannot be implemented when they are are not well publicized. An assistant principal is not able to report this type of offense to an assistant superintendent because in education there is normally a strict chain of command that must be followed. If any teacher or subordinate personnel would try to correct the behavior, he/she would be unsparingly harassed.

If the policy is to be effective, the board of education must make it clearly understood that they will explore the situation so that the guilty personnel will be corrected and the personnel who tried to correct the serious problem will not be punished. School personnel who have problems that indicate alcohol or drug abuse, in most cases, do not understand the depth of their problem, and it will require an experienced counselor to help employees. All forms of correction in education should be used to help a person, not to punish him. Only acts of violence require that we remove a student or school personnel permanently from the school environment.

Alcohol and drug abuse are not the only areas in which public school personnel have gone astray. Unmarried female and male teachers are doing much more than sharing living quarters. Adults have the belief that they can make these decisions, but I believe that the students are aware of many situations, and the teachers' reputations are heavily tarnished. We do not live in a vacuum, and as professionals we should have higher standards because the children will want to emulate our behavior.

The practice of school board members voting as a block has no place in education. In most communities the political party of candidates determines the success that they will have in any election. Since little can be done to change the election process, each individual must decide that he/she will listen to many administrators, teachers, students, and citizens before making a decision and will not be swayed by party politics or a friend's unsupported arguments. The decisions that are made in education have extreme importance on the future of our nation and should not be made unless they reflect what is best for the majority of students. The administration in implementing the policy must provide a support structure for those students who need more assistance in achieving those objectives.

The board of education should also establish an advisory committee to study problems that are presently on the surface and, after solving them, attempt to anticipate areas where future problems can be averted. This committee should be composed of administrators, teachers, citizens, and school board members meeting in an open atmosphere for the purpose of eliminating or solving problems. There is much bitterness during negotiations and during strikes which could be prevented by establishing a committee that can bring unanimous decisions or compromises when considered in an educational type of environment.

Formerly governmental agencies such as the board of education have not been held liable for their torts (wrongful acts subjected to civil suits); however, tort liability has recently become a controversial issue in school law, especially when negligence is involved.

The board of education has the responsibility of defending employees who are doing their job properly, and, should the jury verdict decide against the employee, there are all kinds of moral and legal ramifications. Because the board of education is responsible for policy, legal and administrative assistance must be sought, safety policies adopted, and an education plan implemented which when followed will protect the individuals involved in tort suits. Proper planning will also prevent thousands of dollars from being misused.

Many cases are settled out of court because boards of education do not want to fight the suit in court even though the case would probably be won. Policies submitted by administrations have not been written properly, and others were submitted with the belief that they would not be challenged or that somehow or other the policy would be defended successfully. There are many administrators in education who have no idea of school law, and a board of education that does not do its homework is in my opinion incompetent.

Administrators and teachers are presently being sued for tort liability. The case of *Carroll v. Fitzsimmons*, 384 P. (2d) 81 (Colo. 1963) establishes the fact that an administrator, even though he is not at the scene of the injury stemming from negligence, can be sued and is not immune from torts.

Policies must be established and implemented to minimize if not completely eradicate school district employees from unsuccessful law suits. For example, it is well known that a trampoline is a dangerous piece of equipment when used improperly. The regular physical education teacher is skillful in using teaching techniques, but he is absent and the student teacher and/or substitute teacher has not been taught to use this piece of equipment. When a student gets hurt while using the equipment, the administration will most certainly be liable for their part in

105

the tort occurring in the regular teacher's absence.

As a result of the *Ayala v. School District of Philadelphia*, Pa. 305 A. 2d 877 (1973), Pennsylvania abrogated the doctrine of government immunity. The Court ruled, "If a public official was acting within the scope of his authority and if his conduct was not intentional, malicious, wanton, or reckless he would be considered not liable for negligence." Even if a person is not liable for negligence under this legal ruling, I believe that a lawyer would have a good case in suing the authority who place an irresponsible teacher in that particular situation mentioned above.

Charges have occurred when a physical education teacher matched a large boy in wrestling class against a much smaller boy, when a student was forced to do a front roll on a gym mat, when a playground swing broke, and in hundreds of situations in which the students were unsupervised. Teachers must not force students to perform exercises when they notice that the students are showing fears. The board of education has the responsibility of adopting policies that will protect students from foreseeable risk of harm. Directions must also be given to all employees so that they will have more opportunity to act prudently in all situations.

Boards of Education should seek the recommendations of physicians who have expertise in the area of child development for grades 6-8 if the future of these students is to be protected.

The American Academy of Pediatrics has established guidelines applicable for the elementary and junior high school levels: "Body-contact sports, particularly tackle football and boxing, are considered to have no place in programs for children of this age." [*]

---

[*] Clark A. Bucher, *Administration of Health and Physical Education Programs* (St. Louis: V.C. Mosely Company 1965), pp. 258-259.

Dr. Richard M. Ball, on the faculty of Rutgers University College of Medicine and Dentistry in New Jersey, said,

> Football, in particular, should not be played by the physically immature — the danger of injury by playing too early is great. Boys are mature at about 16 and girls at 14. Before that the growth plates at the end of the long bones are not closed and they must remain healthy if normal growth is to take place. When the skeleton is mature, the growth plates close off and stop.

Ball said a case that outraged him recently involved a high school football star who had injured a wrist. "It was a type of injury I decided to put a cast on. The football coach was outraged that his star couldn't play. He ordered the cast removed. It was taken off so that the boy could play."[*]

If students were more evenly matched physically, there could be more support for tackle football, but even then, a physical development program should be preferred. We are not faced with a decision that forces us to abandon the development of students interested in participating in football nor do we need to continue with the present program which many people believe is a necessity if our students are to compete successfully at the senior high level.

A program that can and should be instituted will consist of the following measures:

First, the physical education program beginning at the elementary level should motivate students to enjoy run-

---

[*]Editorial on 'The Battered Child Athlete', *Medical World News*, as reported by Patricia McCormack, UPI Education Editor in the Daily Local News, West Chester, PA., December 15, 1980.

ning, chasing, fleeing, coordination, throwing, kicking, speed, strength, and endurance development. Nutritional concerns should be coordinated by the nurse and health teachers.

Second, the intermediate school physical education teachers should be capable of developing skills and attitudes that will enhance the student's desire to participate in the physical education and intramural programs.

Third, the football coaches should meet with all interested students each afternoon, at which time running, blocking, form tackling, ball carrying, pass receiving, punting, kicking, passing, pulling, and other football skills are developed. The last part of the practice should be used for touch football and flag football.

The three programs as presented here should provide for the safe development of the twelve-, thirteen-, and fourteen-year-old students going through growth stages so unique that it is unrealistic to expect coaches to understand completely the physiological and emotional status of the students participating at this age level.

The belief is very strong that most middle schools will make necessary changes when they recognize that complete and proper development of most students can take place only when dangerous contact is eliminated and undue stress is minimized. The cardio-vascular system, bone structure, unequal tendon, ligament, and muscular development, and slowly developing coordination can be handicaps unrecognized by coaches. A program that provides for individual differences is a much better curriculum for this unique age group, and the three measures outlined above can provide for the development of those skills and attitudes which will provide more and better athletes interested in playing interscholastic football.

High school coaches believe that middle school students need interscholastic competition in wrestling, basketball, and baseball if high school teams are to be successful in those sports. Educators responsible for the middle school concept generally believe that the students should have a minimum of competition.

Boards of education will have the responsibility of deciding after listening to the arguments. I personally do not believe that the students will be harmed physically, mentally, or emotionally while participating in interscholastic wrestling, basketball, or baseball, but I do believe that the board must consider the financial costs and implement programs accordingly. In education it is important to develop musical, artistic, and athletic talents, not only academic talents. There are many programs that help to develop excellence, and it is the responsibility of administration and supervision to provide the proper choices.

Educators should realize that a student needs an activity in which he/she receives mental as well as physical activity. Mental activity implies much more than a student memorizing a rule book. Athletic activities should include strategies and insights! Each coach should provide situations in which the individual realizes that his thinking process is aiding the team and that he is involved in an activity that requires thinking and judgment.

Very often someone becomes very idealistic and crusades for an extensive intramural athletic program. Unless the board of education is willing to provide bus service, there is very little to be gained by the effort. Instead, an emphasis should be placed on minimizing the cutting of athletes. Actually, some present big league baseball players were cut when they attempted to make the high school baseball team!

Dr. Joseph Torg, a medical doctor who is a leading authority on athletic injuries, stated,

Deaths due to direct cause are those due to trauma directly resulting from participation, such as head injuries and broken necks. Indirect football fatalities are those caused by systemic failure as a result of exercise while participating or by a complication that was secondary to a non-fatal injury. There is one indirect death for each 100,000 players.

The implication for this is that students who are competitive should not be driven to a state of exhaustion in order to reach a certain point of physical condition in a limited time. The teachers responsible for coaching any sport, especially those sports requiring practice sessions during warm weather, must be supervised so that the athletes are getting into condition while they are learning play patterns and skills. Aggressive coaches too often overextend athletes in physical conditioning drills. The coaches have the players believe that they will be the best conditioned team in the country and that this hard work will make them invincible.

Athletes are being pushed unnecessarily, and I hope that your board of education has not permitted this to happen in your community, especially when your son is the one in 100,000 who has died from a coach placing unnecessary stress on him to become invincible.

A professional basketball player received over three million dollars because another professional basketball player punched him in the face. Professional, college, and high school athletes have displayed similar types of physical violence. A board of education that ignores this type of behavior is certainly not competent.

Most educators believe that high school athletes need to be provided with a sport, football, in particular, which permits the student body to support a team activity in

110

competing interscholastically against the athletic team, band, and cheerleaders in another school. Having played college football at the University of Pennsylvania and with the Buffalo Bills in professional football, I would do nothing to discredit football, but I do know that the boards of education can insist on the students receiving the protection that is needed today. Teddy Roosevelt took the step necessary to safeguard football players when he was president of the United States. Now the people have their chance to curb the violence.

STRENGTHS AND WEAKNESSES

Frequently citizens will write letters to the editor of a local newspaper. These letters usually stir up some conversation, but they do not evoke much response. There will be no major changes until citizens demand them, and this will only be accomplished when there is sufficient protest made in your community.

I have asked some citizens to list a few strengths and weaknesses of the public schools.

Dr. Russell Rickert, Dean of Science and Mathematics Department at a Pennsylvania college states:

> There is the absence of a clearly stated goal or purpose. An anecdote may bring the concept of absent goals into focus. I recall clearly attending an "open house" for parents in an elementary school. Teachers and principal reviewed the programs offered and informed the parents about the experiences students were having.
>
> One parent asked, "What are you trying to

accomplish? I mean, what ideal for the children do you have? What do you hope a graduate of your school will be able to do and what would you like him to be?"

Somewhat surprised by the question, the principal replied, "Why, these are your children. We want for them what you want for them."

Is this an informative answer? I suggest that it gave the listeners no information about what that school was trying to accomplish.

There was a time when the society, including the public school system, could enunciate clearly its educational goals. During one period of time, for example, the goal was to prepare children for citizenship in a democratic republic. Much earlier, the goal appeared to be preparation for service to God. Now, the most often heard goal statement goes something like this: "We believe that every child has a right to develop to his or her full potential. This individual, personal development is the real goal of education." Rarely is any mention made of the kind of society in which the person is and will be living; therefore, it is not possible for one to know if the goal is attained.

There are societies in which the goal of education is clearly presented. I've had the privilege of visiting the German Democratic Republic (East Germany). In that country, the primary purpose of all activity is to build the socialistic society. And the leaders have planned the construction process. Of course, the educational system is required to contribute to the accomplishment of this goal. Educators in

113

East Germany openly state that they do not understand how the United States can survive with an educational system which seems to emphasize individual development and disregards the needs of society. Although I do not support the goal or actions of the East German Republic, I acknowledge that their actions are goal-directed.

In my opinion, a society which is unable to state clear goals for itself and its educational system has lost control of its destiny. It is not able to enunciate values: it has no concept of good or bad, of right or wrong, of constructive or destructive actions. Indeed, I believe that the lack of educational goals reflects an overwhelming absence of values, and I could just as well have identified *lack of values* as the foremost deficiency of American Education. But this would not be entirely correct, because it is society which has no values and which has failed to transmit to the educators a goal.

Ann Venable, a mother and teachers' aide, objects to tenure for teachers who aren't capable or interested. She is appalled at the lack of discipline and student concern in some classes. Some tests offered to students are unrealistic, especially in English classes. Many students cannot read comprehensive material. Some teachers swear at the students and provoke bad behavior. The strength appeared to be the opportunity for parents to listen to the teacher's objectives when stated at an "Open House" meeting.

Greg Bowen, real estate salesman, states:

- A better method should be used for selecting teachers and administrators.
- The school environment should be a reasonable facsimile of society, but the parents have not always prepared children to participate in the school's society.
- There are not as many dedicated teachers.
- Standards are being lowered and raised to accomodate students, and the students in the middle are neglected.
- Citizens have yielded their responsibilities to the professional educators.

Dusty Grady, a college student, says:

- Public schools concentrate on the academic and practically ignore the arts, music and art.
- Music offered teamwork, stage knowledge, discipline, duty, a deeper appreciation of culture, strong friendships, and musical knowledge.
- Students can learn more in a supervised class than in a study hall or a free period.

Alice Ebner, teacher's aide, believes:

- Most teachers, programs for special children, and library supervision are impressive.
- Discipline in some classrooms, lack of teacher support, reading and writing skills, and the education available for the average student must receive more attention.

- Disruptive students should be removed from school.
- The school day should be longer to provide for more academic time.
- Tenure should be studied.

Edward Minshall, United Parcel mechanic, makes these points:

- Elective subjects have now replaced important basic subject matter.
- Study of the free enterprise system has been neglected in the schools.
- Only two secondary schools in the nation have tried to teach the private enterprise system.
- The public is leaning toward more government control.
- Student conduct appears to be deteriorating.
- Teachers have no threat to hold over students.
- Parents in defending their children and the general public have hindered behavior patterns of the students.
- Extracurricular activities should help to make many more of the students better citizens.
- Better audio-visual aids today and more aides to assist the teachers are definite strengths.

Ken Kane, science teacher, claims:

- Boards of education should study a twelve-month school year (eliminate flooding of market).

- Twelve-month program gives more time for teacher to develop plans.
- Individualization of instruction, independent study, and talking lounges are helpful.
- Discipline throughout the nation is getting worse because of alcohol and drug abuse.
- General lack of respect is evident.
- Much blame belongs to homes.
- Too many parents are working for luxuries.
- Extracurricular programs should be enlarged to fill needs of secondary students.
- Avocational education is important.
- Moral instruction is needed to help rearrange attitudes.

Ann Calla, mother, says:

- Foreign language is necessary for all well-educated students.
- Average students do not receive training that will enable them to get the skills needed to obtain a job. Students are pushed into curriculum areas because the only vacancies are in those classrooms.
- Typing skills should be introduced for all students.
- Shorthand offers many opportunities.
- Stigma of taking commercial courses should be changed.

Mary Price, mother, preferred to send her children to a school that teaches from a Christian perspective; therefore, her children are attending a private school.

Jay Hess, contract administrator, declares:

- Removing poor and unqualified teachers because of tenure is a serious problem.
- Theory of everyone having an opportunity for an education is good for the country.
- More emphasis on basics is needed.
- New programs appear to be failures.
- Seminar courses appear to always have goals beyond the student's reach.
- Students work harder in seminar courses to get a "B" and other less gifted students make an "A" and get more recognition by taking an easier course.
- Educational research is not the conclusive black and white as developed in scientific research.
- Trial and error has moved education away from the basics.

Paul Munkel, computer manager, says:

- Students who have special types of handicaps are not recognized early enough, if at all.
- Students who work hard in school often have difficulty in obtaining good jobs.
- Teachers are leaving because they receive little support in disciplining students.

A review of these comments evince to me that citizens do have some idea of what is happening in the public schools. Another perspective is that these citizens believe that important changes are necessary. Discipline is a weakness blamed on teachers, administrators, parents,

118

society, homes, and even the students themselves!

The students whom I see in the office are most responsible for the behavior. The parents in ninety-nine out of one hundred cases are embarrassed by the behavior of their child. I will agree that permissive teachers and protective parents at one time or another have enabled the student to act irresponsibly. Parents eventually learned that they were wrong, but I wonder if the administrators will ever inform some teachers that their techniques must be changed.

Emphasis on basics, extracurricular activities, responsibilities to society, employment skills, and establishment of measurable goals are other areas that the citizens recognize as poorly developed.

How much truth is there to the often heard comment that citizens and administrators make: the principal's secretary runs the school! The statement does not portend that education is much of a profession, nor does it signify that administrators have instituted professional objectives. An administrator should be recognized for the classroom observations, for conversations with teachers and students, for helping to maintain better student behavior, and for other professional responsibilities. A principal's secretary should be able to relate information already approved by the administration, and every other teacher and secretary should also be familiar with that information, but she should not be able to make decisions that have any substance in educational areas.

Many teachers are actually afraid of some principals' secretaries! The morale is terrible in these settings because the principal knowingly or unknowingly permits this misdirection to occur. There are also teachers who do not treat secretaries with respect, and this practice is just as unprofessional.

Some teachers are frequently criticized for their ineptitude, and I must again state that the administrators and supervisors have the major responsibility of working with these teachers to improve their teaching techniques. The administrator's other major responsibility is to correct the disruptive students.

In his column, "Our Times," Smith Hempstone stated that Senators George McGovern and Robert Dole are co-sponsoring a bill to establish a National Commission on Literacy. McGovern said,

> Experienced teachers are quitting their jobs in record numbers. The flight is fueled by an intimidating combination of factors — a breakdown of discipline, a deterioration of the instructional process through the endless introduction of pedagogical gimmicks, an unrealistic expansion of public school responsibilities, and, finally, an instinct for self-survival. Physical assaults on teachers now exceed 66,000 annually.[*]

Horrible actions have been displayed by teachers, administrators, and school board members in school districts where I have been employed. These weaknesses and many others can be eliminated whenever the citizens become actively involved in learning more about the public schools and the employees.

A teacher who molested a young female teacher was placed in another school within the district. A few years later the teacher was returned to the same school building and exposed himself to female students and a female member of the teaching staff. No disciplinary action was taken against the teacher, even though students and another teacher suffered this on school property.

[*]Daily Local News, West Chester, Pa., July 27, 1979.

120

A few teachers were very much interested in supporting the candidacy of three school board members. As a reward for their campaigning they were trusting that these three public school board members upon being elected to the school board would vote for the removal of the superintendent of schools, the head varsity basketball coach, and the head varsity football coach! Can you imagine the lack of integrity of these public school board members who would accommodate this degree of irresponsibility?

The superintendent of schools and the principal of the high school informed an applicant that he would be recommended to serve as head football coach. To their chagrin and amazement the board of education at the same time had hired a different teacher to serve as head football coach for the high school! Boards of education have the responsibility of hiring and firing through their voting at a regular or special meeting, but policies must be adopted to define responsibilities and administrative procedures that will eliminate this type of incompetency.

Anyone with any degree of knowledge readily understands that a superintendent of schools or the person he designates will be the only school personnel to have the authority to postpone or cancel school; however, I distinctly recall the president of the school board assuming this responsibility one morning during a snow storm, and you can understand the ludicrous comments concerning this interference with administrative procedures.

A board of education and administration frequently are most unprofessional in supposedly opening up positions for candidates from outside the district and then selecting a person from inside the district who does not have qualifications that are in any degree as suitable as some of the outside candidates'. This practice of allowing outsiders to apply somewhat appeases the board members who believe that the positions should go to the best qualified candidates; however, the board members do not have the courage to question the administrative recommendation.

Some school districts' administrative leaders will not allow former students of that school district to assume any position of leadership nor to return as an employee of that school district! Boards of education should be aware of all candidates because the qualifications of candidates should be the determining factor in placing personnel in positions of leadership. Then in some districts nearly all personnel in leadership and teaching positions are local people, and this situation should also be investigated by a competent board of education.

Principals have been vindictive against candidates who have been hired by superintendents and boards of education because they have believed that they should have the responsibility of hiring all personnel in their school. How can school board members permit this type of jealousy to exist?

Elementary schools have at times made judicious use of parent-teacher associations. The intermediate-level and high schools have not been as willing to allow PTAs to get involved in school affairs. These parent groups should not be money-collecting organizations but should be used in all areas where they can help in providing a better education for all students. Parents who are frequently in the school are more knowledgeable and as citizens must become more involved in insisting on changes which will help to eliminate many of the disruptions that occur daily. Parents should point out weaknesses whenever they exist.

The area of negotiations has been handled very poorly by the board of education and by those appointed to negotiate for the board. Local, state, and federal funds are to be used for salaries, buildings, facilities, materials, transportation, and other areas that function as educational services for pupils.

Many school districts have been inclined to use school district funds in granting severance pay to employees who have worked in the school district for a period of fifteen years or more. Formerly, other co-workers contributed a few dollars to give the retiree a little recognition and a display of gratitude for the contributions that he/she made during the years of service. If there are 600 teachers, supervisors, administrators, and supportive service personnel in your school district, the $50 or $100 granted for each year of service by employees will be an expensive procedure, and I do not believe that money given to provide education for students should be used in any manner not servicing their needs.

A teacher employed by the board of education for a period of thirty years who has taken the properly awarded ten days of sick leave each year has been absent for 300 days. A school year of 180 days is the normal amount of time used for teaching students. A teacher never absent during a similar thirty-year period has actually worked 300 more days, and if he/she has not served in the place of employment for the entire fifteen years would get no severance pay even though the employee has proved to be far more productive and dependable; therefore, even if severance pay is considered morally proper, the policy should be to award dependability, not longevity.

A valuable strength in the teaching, supervisory, and administrative areas is the tenaciousness of the personnel who day in and day out continue to work within the framework established by boards of education which have no idea of the irresponsibility they allow to exist and no conception of the corrective policies that must be adopted to protect the educational rights of all students.

Individual school board members have also worked persistently in trying to get support for policies that they realize could tremendously help the students, taxpayers, and school district. The resistance that they have met has sometimes been overcome, and the school district has been more successful, but important changes will be accomplished only when the board of education adopts additional policies and demands consistent implementation and enforcement of those policies.

Boards of education must demonstrate competency by adopting policies that will require department heads and chairmen to teach a full schedule. Teachers should receive a supplemental contract for performing the duties that help to coordinate the use of books and other classroom resource materials. For example, a chairman receives $18,000. Many schools schedule an eight-period day. The teacher has a period for lunch and another period (usually negotiated or given as a gift) for planning. The five periods required to teach and another period to supervise students in a study hall, cafeteria, or resource room are the real assignments.

If you consider that the teacher is paid $18,000 for teaching and supervising, he is being paid $3,000 for each period. If you release him for three periods to perform coordinating responsibilities, you are really paying $9,000 for those services! If you have twenty department heads, you are using $180,000 for this service each year. Some school boards give the chairmen or department heads released time and additionally pay them a supplemental contract!

I have worked in a school district where the chairman performed this responsibility, and the morale was very good since the position was rotated yearly. No cost, either!

Another program that boards of education allow and that is even more costly because there are more teachers involved is a program in which ten or more teachers meet daily to discuss John's and Mary's classroom behavior! This form of team teaching is most wasteful because very little time is used in perfecting teaching techniques or learning more about the curriculum. If Mary is not interested in learning mathematics, it is the responsibility of the math teacher to motivate her. Students realize that the teacher is unable to help Mary, and as a result many other students will misbehave because they also desire attention or because they realize that nothing bad will happen to them.

Every teacher should be able with proper administrative and supervisory guidance to teach a class successfully. Schools must reject the intermediate school propaganda that attempts to protect these students and is actually harming them and throwing away taxpayers' money. If the boards of education wish to demonstrate competency, they will require the teachers to teach instead of discussing peculiarities of students and their parents.

Instead of paying teachers to attend nonproductive team meetings, assign them to teach more classes, place the disruptive students in a separate classroom from the students who are in school to learn, and require administrators to remove the chronic disruptive students from the classroom or school property.

Education appears to be going downhill so rapidly that there are few older teachers willing to remain in the profession, and many of the younger teachers are already disillusioned with what is taking place. There are many classrooms where good education takes place daily, but there are many, many situations in which a student really desiring to learn is frustrated and literally frightened by what the boards of education allow to happen in the public schools.

Did I hear a board member say, "If you don't like it, get out?" I do like what education was, and I intend to do what I can to help all teachers use teaching strategies free from interference by disruptive students.

Students usually enjoy attending school because they like the socializing opportunities available. They don't like the students who annoy them, and they don't like the teachers who refuse to stop the disturbances. The board of education should not prefer the policies that they have given priority. They have given the students more materialistic objectives and in doing this have failed to institute and develop the citizenship objectives that are necessary if we are to regain our place as the leader in the free world.

A visit to many schools will give you the impression that there was not much thought given to second guessing of the architects who designed the plans for the buildings. Even if the teachers and other school personnel were consulted, I wonder how the final decisions were made. In too many instances the financial costs were overriding. Locker rooms were not provided with lockers, stairways were not wide enough to handle the number of students using them period after period, not enough exits were built to enable students to exit quickly during an emergency, partitions were not thick or flexible enough to provide for various types of teaching approaches, temperature controls were inadequate, gym doors were inoperable, industrial arts areas misplaced, ridiculous room and area combinations were built, and I don't believe one public school board member was fired even though millions of dollars were misused!

Many teachers serve the entire school population because their standards are very high, and they will go out of their way to help resolve a problem that a disruptive student is causing. Other teachers have been offended by administrative decisions and will go out of their way to avoid confrontations. When the board of education demands implementation and enforcement of suitable policies, all teachers will find it necessary to work together in providing a good education for all students.

Barbara Aldin, a parent, made some interesting comments:

> Parents are thankful for the return of the more standard type of teaching as opposed to the open classroom with less teacher instruction and less direct supervision put on the student to finish his work. Students who were not pushed to work in high school did not feel capable of attending college.
>
> There must be more communication between the teacher and the parents. Parents need to be quickly informed when a child is in academic difficulty, and many times the first indication of failure is a poor mark on the student's report card. To contact the teacher appears to be a difficult task because telephone messages are frequently unreturned.
>
> We feel that teacher strikes are completely unfair to the students, there needs to be more discipline in the schools, and there should be better programs offered in the field of special education.

In order to avoid scheduling criticism the public school districts cannot rely on normal computer input. Paul Munkel, an experienced computer manager, blames the computer companies for misleading and only giving partial directions to customers.

I suggest that the public schools require management

to do all scheduling manually, and to furnish the computer companies with accurate complete schedules and additional information so that schools can operate as smoothly during the first few days as they did formerly.

Some boards of education have appointed committees to recommend the best candidate after they have interviewed all candidates; however, committee members are surprised when the board ignores their decision and selects another candidate. Yes, some committees are just appointed with the hope that they'll agree with the board of education's ultimate or, in some cases, a prior decision.

Then there are boards of education that are to make a selection of a principal through a committee of the board members, but it appears that the superintendent of schools actually slants the qualifications of the candidates so that he is the one who really makes the selection and not the board committee which is only a figurehead.

There are school board members who will vote only for local candidates. Can you believe that board members would openly acknowledge that unwarranted position?

It is the responsibility of the board of education to provide available specialists whenever the teaching and administration staffs have agreed that there is a definite learning problem with an elementary school student. It is not necessary that the specialist be a full-time employee, but the services should be available. Hearing, sight, mental, emotional, and other weaknesses must be identified quickly and referred to the proper professional. The professional working with the students who are depressed or overactive should be aware of the problems that can exist whenever the student's chemical makeup is out of balance. Students are more likely to be in need of a proper diet, multivitamins, and medication than they are of counseling. Secondary students have a difficult time coping with depression, and counseling will not be of much help if the student's mind is not functioning properly. Students who have committed suicide were probably regarded as merely unhappy by their parents.

Teachers and administrators make thoughtless comments. There is a need for all professionals to think of the consequences before they offer comments to students. In describing sex, a teacher said that it is like dancing: you can do it better if you practice! A teacher remarked that a girl looked very good in her sweater. What was intended as a compliment had various interpretations by the time it reached the school board.

A teacher informed the students that they were mature enough to make all of their own decisions and that the parents should understand this. Well, all parents did not agree with this philosophy, and again the story reached the school board. A couple of teachers instructed students in health classes that they realized that the students would be having intercourse and then advised them to buy contraceptives so that there would be no problem! Another teacher told all of her students that everyone does something because it will profit them. For example, a person goes to church because he wants to be seen there. Yes, some people might go to church because they want to be seen there, but to make a blanket statement like this to students who respect you is taking unfair advantage of the people who go to church for the purpose of worshipping God and for serving other people who wish to follow the teachings of God.

Armchair decision makers are plenteous in the public schools. A principal did not leave his office because of his weak heart. He got his information from Harry, the custodian! In doing repairs and cleaning Harry was able to observe what was happening throughout the school. The questions that the principal asked me could only be asked by someone who had observed me personally, and, since the custodian was the only visitor, I knew that my evaluator was a custodian! The principal admitted that the custodian had been the observer. I told the principal that the teaching techniques were taught to me by professors at the University of Pennsylvania and that, even if the methods were not the same as used by the teacher who had taught previously, they were working successfully for me and that I would prefer that the principal see them in operation before he passed judgment.

Another administrator whom I worked for also had a physical ailment which severely hampered the work that he was able to do, even though a year or two before he had the use of a very keen mind and body strength. At that time I felt only compassion for him, but in retrospect I believe that a professional should resign or step-down to a less important position whenever he is not mentally or physically capable of performing in the higher position in an outstanding manner.

Too many people in the public schools want to mold other people into their own image. I worked with a department chairman who told me that I was one of two or three teachers doing things differently than the other thirteen people in the English department, and that he wanted to have all teachers use the same teaching techniques. Look out, 1984, here we come! Since this was suggested in the 1960s I did not believe that I should be required to forgo all of my individual thinking, and luckily I survived.

Parents send their sons and daughters to the public schools believing that the school boards are interested in providing conducive learning environments, but there are very few available! The communities that are permitting children and young adults to threaten, molest, and pummel people are the same communities that permit the school to be arenas of verbal challenges and physical combat.

Your sons and daughters should be the most beloved and valuable possessions in the schools. Parents rightfully expect schools to protect children. When someone mistreats the children at home, the parents will at least try to do whatever is necessary for protection: however, even though they realize that the school boards and school personnel are not doing the job properly, parents appear to be willing to live with the problems.

When I became a teacher in 1948, teaching was a dignified profession. The schools lost dignity the moment that the teachers and administrators permitted students to challenge their authority and responsibility. Students disturb the teachers by talking, and, when asked to be quiet and/or move to another seat, they sarcastically begin to question the intelligence and sexual preferences of the teachers! Students screaming in hallways and annoying other students refuse to obey the teachers, curse the teachers, and refuse to identify themselves.

Students will continue to abuse other students physically and to challenge teachers because one or two days of detention or suspension is not the proper disciplinary measure for school boards to adopt. School personnel are negligent in pointing out to the school boards that you cannot have good public schools unless the insubordinate students who threaten and defy teachers are placed in alternative environments or expelled from the schools. You will discover that very few students will challenge authority when they understand that this will not be tolerated. Students and teachers must recognize that asking more questions about the course content is to be encouraged but that students must not attempt to ridicule teachers.

Teachers must be consistent in referring all violators to administrators. Many students complain that teachers are

131

afraid of some students and in being this way permit these students to annoy other students physically and educationally. Can you imagine the stresses that teachers experience when these rebellious students challenge and defy them? Defiances occur often in such a manner, usually, that the teachers learn to adjust to the rudenesses by ignoring them! Other teachers who object to the belligerent actions are accused of prejudice. These teachers realize that the policies of the public schools suggest that the teachers cope with classroom minor disturbances! When the usurping of authority became a minor disturbance, the public school authorities took their places among the permissive judges, legislators, parents, and laymen who consider the individual's rights more important than the rights of the majority of students who are being abused mentally, physically, emotionally, and educationally.

School boards do have the right and the responsibility to mandate policies that will remove disruptive and threatening students from the schools. Administrators must implement these policies by insisting that all teachers follow policies. Students who believe that teachers are abusing authority should have the courage to report these actions to administrators. Yes, there are teachers whose behavior must be modified.

Is it too unreasonable to believe that there are many mean, tough, vicious, and dumb students in the public schools who are a physical threat to your children and who are regularly preventing teachers from using appropriate teaching techniques? Before you believe your administrations and school boards, read the policies and question the teachers and students concerning the behavior of the disruptive students. If you do not receive remedies, there are many forms of exposure that can be used to help your teachers to begin to teach. I say, "Let them teach again — without interruptions."

School board members should witness an angry (closer to mad) seventeen-year-old trying to kill another student because an extremely mild incident ignited him. Teachers and administrators are legally bound to control that student with a minimum of force. What do you think happens to the student being struck when the teacher is not stronger than the "killer"? Should the teacher be beaten too, or should he/she run for help?

School boards should set policies to remove violent students immediately from the schools. Students who use violence are a constant threat to other students. Most children stay out of their way, and other students "back down." Sometimes violent students won't let you walk away from them!

In the late 1960s, Plainfield High School, Plainfield, New Jersey, took much discretionary power away from the principals when the authorities decided that a jury of students and teachers would render verdicts after they directly heard the evidence from the teachers reporting students for smoking or for other school violations and after hearing the statements offered by the students who are defending themselves.

Can you imagine the enormous amount of time required to implement this type of procedure? The administrators favoring this procedure said that they did not want to see an administrator acting as a god!

The teachers with whom I spoke stated that they would never turn in a student for a violation that occurred outside their classrooms because they did not feel that the amount of time involved in charging a student with a violation was worth the detention or day's suspension that the student might receive.

A similar way-out course was also in vogue in this area at that time. A "sensitivity course" was intended to teach

each adult to learn to relax and at the same time be much more expressive in allowing the other person to know that we were really "cool" and could communicate with him or her very affectionately. I sometimes wondered how the spouse would have reacted when he or she saw the final session in which there was much hugging and kissing going on! I guess that releasing of energy was the ultimate test. Nevertheless, this type of expression is a little difficult to incorporate into a discipline practice for the public schools, especially at the secondary and middle-level schools.

In New Jersey you must have a superintendent even if you only have one school! The superintendent was responsible for having other employees do budgeting and transportation. He did hire all employees. In fact, he was a business manager because the principal and his two assistants were responsible for administering the one and only school. The three school districts sending students to the high school each had a superintendent of schools for two or three very small elementary schools. The entire school system needed one superintendent instead of four superintendents. When you pay four superintendents, you are talking about a lot of money because each one would have business managers and secretaries. The taxpayers permitted this lavish waste of tax money and the local school boards were fighting to maintain local autonomy even though the high school teachers discovered that in teaching the students from the three sending minidistricts that no one district was preparing the students any better than the other two districts.

Two administrators sent to another state to observe an educational program were informed by the superintendent that he did not want the school board to know that this was happening or that he was aware of the visitation.

Custodians must receive orientation concerning deportment, and they must also receive daily supervision in their relationships with students. Students have been cursed and physically abused. The custodians when apprehended have been fired or moved to other schools.

A school board member's wife telephoned to argue that her son's bus should not be scheduled to arrive at an earlier time. She was informed that at mid-year bus arrivals would be changed so that all students would be treated equally. She did not agree with this philosophy (nor did her husband).

The president of the school board interceded in defending a student who had been removed from riding a school bus after the student had hit the woman bus driver by throwing eggs at her. Guess who was able to ride the school bus immediately?

An assistant superintendent telephoned to say that his daughter was not going to be given detention or a suspension even though the teacher said that the girl had deliberately kicked another student. Guess who was not disciplined?

An administrator was told that a part-time employee was to be dropped from the payroll. The administrator complained that the employee appeared to be doing a satisfactory job and that the timing for removal was very poor. The instructions were to comply. The administrator acted immediately and in doing so discovered much mystery and intrigue that he had never heard before. Oh, yes! The administrator was criticized for dropping the employee!

Most administrative decisions are easy to make because most teachers use patience and considerate deliberation in correcting a misbehaving student. Other teachers multiply a small problem in the process of handling a discipline referral. The school personnel who yell at students, tell them to "shut up," unnecessarily grab them, or challenge students place the administrators in a most sensitive position. Students, according to law and proper human logic, are equal to adults and must be treated as the adults expect other people to treat them. Administrators must support teachers, but we find it most difficult to convince students that the teacher is allowed to treat them as less than human, and yet the students get punished for the same type of behavior.

One of my former students and athletes, Lou Falzarano, Millington, New Jersey, after returning home from one of his semesters at Notre Dame University suggested to me that teachers should never make a rule unless it will help people. When, as happens very often, a problem arises with only one student, that problem should be resolved with that person. It is senseless to antagonize students who have no intention of breaking any rule and do not want a teacher to label them as potential troublemakers.

College professors have defended the practice of the administration's hiring and firing. I will agree that the administration is responsible for supervising and evaluating the employee's daily performance, but I am not in accord with the theory advanced by professors when it is much more logical and democratic to place the hiring of personnel and the establishment of all policies in the hands of the nine school board members. When nine school board members can sit down to discuss hiring of personnel and selection of policy, they can debate and through a consensus be more consistent in making the correct decisions. An autocratic decision should never replace a consensus whenever major decisions are to be made.

Even though the law requires the full board to vote on policy, the West Chester Area School District Superintendent has adopted a unique method of providing a place for an administrator or supervisor on each committee;

therefore, whenever a discipline, personnel, finance, curriculum or other committee of the board meets, the board members are able to ask questions and to receive information from someone who is normally familiar with the problems in those areas.

A school board that implements these committees must be careful that the employee is not penalized for expressing valid concerns during these meetings because many superintendents and assistants are most reluctant in allowing subordinates to give information directly to school board members! In fact, there are many administrators who would be most vindictive if a subordinate spoke to a board member about anything, especially an education matter!

The administration should remind other professionals that, if they are to lead students in listening attentively, then they should try to condition themselves to this evidence of courtesy by maintaining silence among themselves when they are in an assembly or meeting.

I recall a superintendent of schools who required all members of the administration and teachers to meet with him prior to meeting with the board so that the school board wouldn't hear something that the superintendent did not want them to hear! The practice is common.

In contrast to this type of leadership I respect my leaders who have helped employees when they were ill or without a job because they realized that these employees went beyond their normal assignment to help the students in the school district. The leaders who show compassion have been able to get loyalty from most employees.

An administration that is so anxious to protect all professionals and other employees from student abuse should be just as eager to inform teachers that they should not abuse students physically, mentally, emotionally, or socially.

A few years ago many hearings were held by the U.S. Supreme Court so that citizens could present arguments concerning the wisdom of removing scripture and prayer from the public schools. Many ministers, priests, members of Congress, educators, and other citizens will find it difficult to prove that they were wise in arguing to remove God from any area of our society, especially the public schools! The attorney general in all states has not found it necessary to remove what was once certainly the will of the majority of our citizens. Today many students never hear a word about God inside the school or in the community.

Buck Jones, youth director and college math major, believes that public school facilities, extracurricular activities for social needs, exposure to new ideas, and the opportunity to interact with students possessing different lifestyles are advantages of attending the public schools.

Most students told him that gym and lunch are their favorites! This answer is a sad commentary on the academic classrooms. In large measure teachers have failed to work at creating a positive learning atmosphere in the classrooms. There is often little variety in lesson planning. The teacher only checks homework, might present new material, and then assigns more problems.

When a history teacher verbally reprimanded a sixth grade student, the student snapped back, "If you touch me, my father will sue you!" The public schools appear to be unable to enforce discipline. The teachers, administrators, students, and laymen have the attitude, "What can I get?" They should assume the attitude, "What can I give?"

Mr. Jones is critical of teachers' behavior. He said, "There is the mistaken notion that one can be a good teacher regardless of the lifestyle lived outside the classroom. Instead, the lifestyle filters through to the students in the classroom, and the students reflect rebellion in their attitudes."

The lifestyles mentioned by Buck Jones are frequently not well hidden by the teachers, and the students will comment on what they believe to be immoral.

The board of education in most situations will not want to get involved in this although students do not respect the teacher when he has acted irresponsibly, and certainly immorality, when continued, definitely must be eliminated even if it means dismissal of the teacher.

The remark of the sixth grade student who snapped at the teacher is typical of the student who is in a school district in which the board of education has eliminated corporal punishment. When a board of education takes away this option, the student realizes that he/she can say anything and the suspension, detention, or reprimand will be more acceptable to him than the possible embarrassment if he had been given a solid crack with the paddle; therefore, he feels no real restraint.

Under no circumstances should it be necessary to give a student more than one crack, and in most cases a conversation between the administrator and the student might indicate that a suspension would be a better deterrent.

An administrator should not give the student a crack with the paddle unless, in his judgment, it is necessary. The board of education must permit corporal punishment under the proper circumstances. Students must understand that the teacher will not be verbally abused.

Many students pass through all grades without peer friendship. Teachers, counselors, and administrators must discover and help these students early so that the students with drug abuse and truancy tendencies will not have the opportunity to entice them into joining their groups.

Some school board members have been correct in maintaining an affirmative action program. If the policy is to seek candidates who can equal or surpass the candidates who have been applying, then the practice is most worthwhile. If the practice is to achieve a quota, especially when it interferes with other educators' constitutional rights, the tactic is a disgrace and must be stopped.

The most successful minority students have proved that their abilities are just as high. The average achieving minority students are just as successful as the average achieving majority students. The lowest achieving minority students and the students with the worst behavior patterns have many counterparts among the majority students. If the objective is equality, and this intent has already been demonstrated by the students who really want to be equal, then please ignore the radicals who are still crying about inequality. If someone is denying any student equality, please point out the educator for corrective purposes, but don't cry "wolf" and embarrass the minority educators who have been doing a terrific job.

And please forget the racial references. Students usually understand how educators feel about them. I'm sure that there are many of us who can see only the human race and can only hope that the unhappy people can learn the truth about God's love and will for all people.

Homogeneous grouping has been used in many intermediate public schools for years. This practice has immensely pleased many of the teachers because the planning requires minimum attention, and there are many more moments offered for teachers to relax.

The outstanding or "A" students are all placed in the same classroom section. The "B" students or those slightly above average in achievement are placed in a second section. The "A" and "B" sections have some opportunity for classroom discussion if the teacher selected to teach them is able to handle the questions that some sagacious students project. The average, below average, and very slow students are placed in the lower three sections, and these students are engaged in busy work! If you give any thought to what I have just stated, you will understand that sixty percent of the students will have very little opportunity for discussion and absolutely no opportunity to listen to the interesting questions and answers that the "A" and "B" type students use in their much more stimulating learning environment.

Superintendents and school boards who have taken the steps to eliminate this form of homogeneous grouping should be congratulated for overcoming the unfair practice that stupid administrators allowed to exist because they were pressured by a small but vocal minority. Even the "B" type students never had an opportunity to experience the advantages of learning in a classroom with students who at this stage of education were more gifted. It could be safely argued that 80 percent of the students were not receiving an education comparable to that received by the students in the "A" section. Some parents were well aware of the unfairness, and they applied pressure until their children were placed in a more favorable section. It is very hard for me to believe that public school board members would be so inconsiderate of student rights and school board responsibilities as to permit this to happen.

Althought it was not my official responsibility, I called central office to inform them that one of our bus drivers had been stopped by the police department for speeding, and I felt that they should be informed of the fact. The next morning the person in central office assigned to bus transportation came to the school and informed me that the bus driver was experienced in the school district and that he knew nothing about me since I was a new administrator! He informed me very rudely that the students on the bus were very unruly and that is why the bus was stopped. I informed the gentleman that the police had called me, and an officer had told me that the driver was speeding. This could be easily checked. My story was confirmed. I have used this incident to illustrate one of the many ridiculous occurrences that take place in the public schools regularly.

Some educators are adamant in defending the retention of students who are not able to master all of the subject matter in the intermediate school. What these educators completely ignore is the threat that these retained students are to the other students in their classes. Students who are one and a half to two years older should not be held back if they are or can potentially become a physical threat. Students in the intermediate-level schools are not in self-contained classrooms but are scheduled to take courses in different classroom and teaching areas throughout the school day.

The looseness of the structure and the inabilities of the teachers and administrators frequently enable retained students to frighten other students in the school physically and emotionally. If these students were to be moved along with students who are near the same age chronologically until they reached the ninth grade level, the other students would by that time be more able to defend themselves from the abuses that they are not able to handle in lower grades. In a secondary setting there are many upperclassmen whose physical presence also deters the threatening antics of the class bullies.

School board members must recognize that all students must have a clearly stated discipline guide that informs them that class cutting, classroom disturbances, and other forms of irresponsibility will not be tolerated. It is a fact that students who want to remain in school will not step beyond the limits established for them. Educators must be consistent in enforcing. If educators fail to do this, the students will continue to lead teachers and administrators on the merry-go-round that only goes in circles, never forward.

Rebellious students do not want to be in school, but, since they are required to be there, they will think of many and various ways to convince other students to hide in lavatories, lunch rooms, and social study halls.

If members of the school board give this unstructured liberty to hundreds of students who are not able to function unless they have a solid structure to guide them, they are actually harming hundreds of students in order to keep a couple of students in school who are a serious emotional threat to the teachers responsible for controlling them in the classroom.

Internal suspension should certainly be offered to those students who have violated school regulation three or four times, but, when you consider that a school provides a teacher to supervise a violator for fourteen days of internal suspension at taxpayers' expense, it is then certainly time for the parents to furnish supervision.

The administrators and counselors must yield most of their working hours in chasing and counseling a few students who do not want to be in school. These students realize that we are sincere in attempting to make school more meaningful for them, but they are unwilling or unable to function in a public school at this time. Endeavors should be made to place these students who cannot function in a normal manner with teachers who can achieve success with most youngsters. However, when these teachers have tried unsuccessfully, the students must be expelled from school so that the remaining students can receive more professional assistance and the teachers can receive supervision fully intended to improve instruction.

School board members must select the right priorities and policies if they intend to demand school personnel to be accountable. Although accountability is practiced in many school districts, the disruptive students continue to misbehave and the teachers are under constant pressures.

Secondary school assistant principals are in the most advantageous position among all school personnel to understand what is happening in the public schools because every day the assistant principals' responsibilities take them into all areas where students and teachers venture. Other administrators, supervisors, and teachers have assignments that do not include the opportunities that assistant principals have to observe interactions.

Many administrators, supervisors, teachers, and college professors have proposed programs and gimmicks which were tried and did very little to improve education. The recommended programs and more money are not good solutions.

School districts can accomplish little by using patchwork mending and other forms of uncoordinated attempts. One person cannot administer the needed revisions, but all school districts should have enough personnel for a successful coordinated effort.

A successful educational program will have:

- consistent discipline by teachers and assistant principals;
- both innovative and structured teaching techniques;
- dedicated, understanding, and knowledge-

able teachers;
- administrators who visit classrooms and other teaching areas;
- intelligent, challenging, and studious school board members; and
- aggressive and result-oriented laymen.

The school board and laymen must establish the priorities listed above so that all public school students receive an outstanding education. Don't let anyone sell you on a long-term contract; a team effort can get results in less than one school semester.

CONCLUSIONS

Many teachers are living under unnecessary stress every day that they report to work. Teachers who have been very successful in the field are leaving because they believe that the school environment is getting worse daily. There are other teachers who would like to leave but are not qualified to enter a business market which bears all indications of a recession. The teachers who are leaving are not normally entering positions that will provide them with a higher salary. No, these teachers are leaving because they do not like the direction in which education is headed.

The disruptive student is in all schools, and he/she will continue to act out hostility, strive for attention via irrational means, and craftily upset nearly everything that a teacher attempts to do. As long as a teacher feels insecure concerning job security and as long as the administrators refuse to demand proper behavior in the classroom, the disruptive student will continue to enjoy his/her adventures.

A student discipline guide may look good on paper, but how is it implemented? Boards of education appear to take great pride because students have not been expelled from school. It would certainly be a great experience to teach in a school where all of the students are so well behaved that they all belong in school! Teachers in all schools will readily inform you that there are many students who do not belong in school as a result of their present behavior. Many of these students would belong in school if the administrators would work to correct the behavior patterns, but the attitude appears to be that the problems aren't that important. Administrators, the teachers do not believe you!

A student discipline guide must list the possible violations and the firm disciplinary actions taken for all intentional violations. In addition to this, though, the administrators must visit classrooms daily to give the teacher the support that is needed to protect the rights of the students who are in school for an education.

Vandalism and theft do cause school districts to lose funds that could be utilized for educational purposes. Some school districts have set aside money usually lost on vandalism and have given students the opportunity to use the money for class projects whenever the vandalism has been minimized. Students have splashed paint on teachers' cars, made large dents, placed nails in tires, and cracked windows after a teacher has been critical of their behavior. An administrator who is doing his job well will be able to apprehend, suspend, and collect damages from those students because the other students will identify the violators for an administrator whom they like.

Demanding parents are good for any school district because they do keep educators informed of problems. Parents who are demanding a special individualized educational program for their children certainly are taking the right step in their demands, and the gifted program will probably have some degree of success when it becomes implemented properly. My contention is that all students should have a gifted education and will have it when the disruptive student is corrected and the teacher then has an opportunity to use the best teaching techniques with guidance offered by supervisory and administrative personnel.

Fear, insecurity, and pressure are brought about in many areas in which the teacher has not been supported by the supervisor or administrators.

Teachers fear that they will be physically assaulted by students or intruders on school premises. They fear that they will be evaluated under circumstances that they have little power to control. They feel the insecurity of their teaching position because the enrollment decrease will mean that teachers will be dropped and there is no indication in which departments this will occur. The evaluators are in the classrooms only once or twice a year, and there is the pressure of figuring out what the evaluators expect of a teacher.

Pressures can be discipline, family, health, relatives, term papers, personality clashes, or any number of other problems that affect the lives of all citizens.

The salary issue should be decided by the local board of education. The normal person in the teaching profession is not capable of working two jobs and he/she should receive proper increments year after year for possessing experience under a capable administration. There is no logical or reasonable explanation for a board of education to pay administrators and supervisors the enormous differences in salary when the responsibilities and decision-making factors are analyzed in relationship to those of the teachers in the school.

Administrators and supervisors are entitled to more

pay whenever they support extracurricular programs or complete work when students leave the building. Administrators have to endure physical confrontations in removing intruders, separating fighters, and controlling drug and alcohol abusers. Someone must discipline the violent students, and it is not a supervisor, nor is it usually a teacher.

Evaluations are an exercise in futility or subjectivity. The objective form of evaluation which is necessary will be possible when the teacher can use appropriate teaching techniques. Today the disruptive student limits this day after day.

The objective evaluation must determine the value of the teacher's preparation, teaching techniques used for mastering the objectives, and the student reaction throughout the period. This can be accomplished objectively when an evaluator is in the classroom for six hours or the equivalency of a day's teaching assignment.

The board of education will insist on a fair number of administrative offerings placed on the agenda if the members are to make the best possible decision in adopting a policy. If the administrators want to implement a reading program, they should submit three or four reading programs with their strengths and weaknesses listed so that the board of education can make a decision more objectively.

The curriculum should not be changed every year in the form of a new curriculum guide. The curriculum, if properly adopted, should be a solid one in which the teacher can make necessary adjustments during the period for group or individual differences and still be reaching the major objectives necessary for the student to acquire during the immediate school year.

The instructional program should not be based on a new model but should be centered around the teacher using every talent at hand to offer his/her knowledge to a classroom in which there is much interaction. At times too much money is used for buildings, facilities, and bus transportation. Boards must select more practical buildings and endeavor to produce better bus routes.

Do not be influenced by the weak board members and unscrupulous lawyers who contend that the public school must educate all students in a normal public school environment. There are students who will interfere with the teaching and learning daily. Guidelines must be adopted to set limits for these violators, and the administrators are to be responsible in following these guidelines.

The permissive attitude that was dominant in the 1960s is prevalent today, and society must effect changes since many school boards do not have enough intelligence or courage to defend an outstanding educational environment.

Some readers will remember that they had the opportunity to attend schools where they could attend classes controlled by the teacher. Today there are classes that have a few students who will not remain silent so that the teacher can use various teaching techniques. The teacher is "holding the lid on" and using a modified technique that is better suited for disciplining than for teaching. Some teachers comment after being observed teaching that they were disappointed in not getting more credit for the lesson, especially since the students were much better behaved during that period of observation. Naturally, the students would not interfere with the lesson when an administrator was in the classroom, but this statement also implies that the students are disturbing the teaching/learning environment whenever an observer is not in the room.

Boards of education throughout the United States are now striving for accountability. Unless the standards and policies are appropriate, accountability only touches the surface. My contention is that boards of education are shirking their main responsibility: to provide teaching/learning environments in which teachers can use the right techniques and materials and the learners understand that they can learn much more from a teacher who is not sidetracked by disruptive students.

I have had the pleasure of working with many outstanding teachers, administrators, and school board members. Three female school board members were very aggressive in attempting to correct some of the many weaknesses that exist in all school districts. Even though boards of education are top-heavy with male members, I do not believe that after serving for thirty-two years in public schools as a teacher or as an administrator that I can name many men who really researched what was taking place in the schools! Granted that many board members would study the handouts issued by school district personnel concerning finances and statistics tailored to make personnel look good, but the more important areas of supervision of instruction, curricula, student behavior, needs of the normal students, and job performances have received superficial attention.

School board members are not city council members! Council members are there to protect the taxpayers' wallets by voting intelligently on financial costs for police, firemen, water supply, sewerage, and other public services. School board members are elected for the prime purpose of seeing that an outstanding educational program is offered to all students, and there is no way that board members can do this unless they visit the schools on unguided tours. The scheduled visits are not appropriate for learning what is really happening.

Some school board members have used their position as a stepping stone for a political career. Some people

151

have "axes to grind" for use against administrators, coaches, and teachers. Some people just want to "belong," and other people are there to represent "special interests." I do believe, however, that there are many good board members who will become active whenever they realize that they do have a more meaningful purpose in serving on the boards of education for the public schools. Because there is no perfect school district, the need for your direction is necessary in all communities.

School board members in the vast majority of cases are good people in the community who devote much of their time and energy in attempting to serve the needs of the students, teachers, administrators, and the public. These citizens serve without pay and in many situations receive much verbal abuse and derision in defending what they believe to be right. There is no doubt that this same majority will be receptive to constructive criticism and are probably already working to adopt more appropriate policies.

Teaching will be much easier when administrators rearrange priorities and decide that disruptive students, teaching techniques, and the educational curricula for all students deserve immediate attention and some resemblance of stability.

Athletic coaches should be allowed to encourage all athletes to develop their skill abilities throughout the year provided that this encouragement does not restrict the athlete in developing talents in other athletic activities. The emphasis in athletics should be to eliminate those coaches who are more concerned with victory than with the safety and health of the athlete. Only board of education pressure can eliminate the face mask, which causes football to be a game of violence, not a sport.

The American citizen must understand that there is no

mystic, no overwhelming problems in public education, but there is a need for all members of boards of education to work toward competency by insisting that administrators, supervisors, and teachers do the job that the public rightfully expects them to be doing.

Let's rate your school board according to how well they meet the ten responsibilities listed below under their usual standards: O - outstanding; VG - very good; G - good; S - satisfactory; and U - unsatisfactory:

1. Requires administrative recommendations to list suitable alternatives.
2. Feels pulse of educational climate by talking to teachers, students, and other personnel.
3. Visits schools unannounced to get a real picture instead of a guided tour.
4. Visits classrooms, cafeteria, and study halls to observe student behavior.
5. Demands daily work schedules to be followed by supervisors and administrators.
6. Expects supervisors, administrators, and central office personnel to participate in community activities.
7. Understands via observations and conversations the character of coaches and other extracurricular sponsors.
8. Requires administrators and supervisors to visit classrooms daily.
9. Requires principals to prove that the curriculum and instructional program are meeting the needs of all students.
10. Adopts policies supporting the teachers and administrators in removing disruptive students from the classroom.

When school board members climb down from their ivory towers and implement these responsibilities, they will no longer be incompetent.

Superintendents have been hand-picking principals, assistant principals, and supervisors throughout the years. Therefore, nearly everything that occurs in education has happened before, and, even though needs of students change every year, there has and will be very few adjustments to compensate for these needs. It is most essential that board of education members become active in hiring key personnel.

The laymen should understand that:

1. Board of education members must make important decisions concerning policies and personnel. A discipline code must be established that will define the punishment for repeated classroom confrontations.
2. The superintendent of schools is responsible for submitting all major policies and information along with recommendations. He must supervise all administrators and supervisors.
3. The principal is responsible for the administration and supervision of the school curricula. The curricula should be varied enough to provide a good education for all students. The principal is to evaluate all staff members.
4. Assistant principals are responsible for giving support to the teachers and students by correcting the misbehavior of disruptive students. Assistant principals observe teachers for the purpose of improving instruction.

5. Teachers are responsible for using a variety of techniques in an endeavor to help all students. Teachers must get involved in assignments beyond the regular classroom.
6. Students have the responsibility of obeying all school regulations and policies. Students who interfere with the teaching/learning environment must be temporarily and then permanently removed from the public school.
7. The layman who has attended school is capable of judging sound educational programs because he has experienced good and poor programs, techniques, and approaches. The layman should be familiar with the educational programs and personnel in the local schools and should insist on all employees producing instead of hiding behind the shield that says, "I'm a professional. I have expertise. I have tenure. How dare you question my ability?"

The purpose of this book has been to identify the major weaknesses in the public school system and to offer stated or implied solutions for each of the weaknesses. The weaknesses will be better understood whenever the board members enter the schools and observe the happenings firsthand.